CYBERSECURITY NOW

CRUCIAL STRATEGIES FROM 11 IT SECURITY PROFESSIONALS NATIONWIDE

Prominence Publishing
www.prominencepublishing.com

Cybersecurity Now/Chris Wiser. -- 1st ed.
ISBN: 978-1-988925-75-2

Contents

Foreword

By Chris Wiser

As we look back on 2020, there are many things we have learned, and one thing holds true for every business owner: preparing for the unknown is crucial to business longevity. Last year brought a level of uncertainty to the business community that threatened business owners worldwide. Entrepreneurs around the world had to change their business model and the way they had been operating for years. Through this uncertainty, I have learned much about my own business; specifically, I always need a plan for adapting to various circumstances and how to survive the unknown.

Business owners who chose to adapt to the unknown, planned and strategized for growth, and then implemented and executed those strategies had greater success than those business owners that chose to do nothing but "ride it out". This was a huge life lesson in and of itself.

Through our work, we helped managed service providers continue to grow during 2020. As a community, we learned that cybercrime played a crucial role in the business community over the course of last year. As we may remember, the COVID-19 pandemic changed the business model, forever altering the way most businesses operate. We saw an unprecedented increase in the number of businesses that supported remote workforces and the need to secure these businesses against threats from the outside world. Most of my clients learned that business owners were not placing an emphasis on securing their business assets, but rather concentrating on how they could continue to operate efficiently through the pandemic. When I think about the growing number of businesses that now support a remote workforce but are not properly secured it makes me think what a massive issue this has become across the entire business community. How many businesses are being exposed to hackers right now? How many business owners even care?

Many business owners understand what cybersecurity "is", but never quite understand the need for it. The fact of the matter is, cyberattacks affect all people associated with your business and are so common these days, that not properly securing your business network leaves your confidential information and business assets at risk. Business owners are not only exposing their own personal information, but also the personal information of every employee and client they have or had.

It is no surprise that cybersecurity should be a crucial part of every business as we have seen a huge increase in cybercrime over the course of the year – just open your web browser and type in "cyberattack near me" and see what you find...

We can no longer turn our cheek and look the other way when businesses neglect to secure their business assets. It's not only the personal and confidential information of every employee and every client, but it's also associated sensitive business information you would not want leaked to the public.

During a time of crisis, it's understandable that some business owners opt to take the easy way out and not secure their business because they are just trying to keep their heads above water, but we have learned through 2020 this is NOT a good idea. Cybersecurity is no longer an option to have in your stack and, as an MSP business owner, it should no longer be an option to support clients that deny cybersecurity. Cybersecurity is not a commodity – instead, cybersecurity is essential for every business owner and it is our job to convey this to the business community. As managed service providers, it is your job to educate the business community about the importance of cybersecurity and the NEED for securing the information within their business.

In this book, we have brought together eleven IT security experts to help business owners understand WHY Cybersecurity matters, and what needs to be done NOW, before it's too late. We do not want to see yet another small business close because they did not take the right steps to secure their IT network and safeguard their confidential assets.

Chris Wiser,

CEO, 7 Figure MSP

Speaker/Trainer/ Entrepreneur Coach

The Best Defense is a Good Offense

By George McCracken

A few years ago, we had a client that was unwilling to listen. We met with them regularly and stressed the need to improve their security and backups. Each time the response was, "The IT provider you took over from never had an issue and neither should you. We'll be fine." What should you take away from that response? First, we were taking over from another IT provider that this client was not happy with. One of the main reasons for the dismissal of the previous provider was that the client felt surprised by issues that came up and didn't feel enough planning was in place. Second, the client was relying on information provided to them by a provider that wasn't meeting their needs.

If I knew then what I know now, I would have never taken them on as a client. The business was run by very good people who are considered, in our area, real experts in their field. However, they were comfortable. Too comfortable.

Our help desk received a call from this client sometime later and said that many of the files on their main file server were no longer accessible. They could see the files, but when you tried to open them, nothing happened. The client was officially a victim of a form of crypto locker, malicious software that encrypts the files on any attached network-accessible drive so that the user can no longer access the files. I can't tell you the pain in the eyes of my clients as the two of us watched the files being encrypted and changed right before our eyes.

The moral of the story is this: if the client had taken the advice of a trusted resource and proactively put things in place, this never would have happened. It took weeks and thousands of dollars to recover from the issue and some of the data was lost forever. Forever... let that sink in.

Fast forward to today and it's clear to see that proactive cyber defense is no longer something that should just be discussed. It needs to be implemented yesterday. Before diving deeper into proactive cyber defense itself, here are some basic things all small business owners should know about the current cybersecurity landscape:

- 43% of all cyber-attacks target small businesses

- 60% of small businesses that are victims of a cyber-attack go out of business within six months

- From September 2019 through September 2020, there was a 424% increase in new small business cyber breaches

- Human error and system failure account for 52% of all data security breaches with 63% of confirmed data breaches are enabled by the use of weak, default, or stolen passwords

- 54% of small businesses think they're "too small" for a cyber-attack

- Small businesses spend an average of $950,000 to restore normal business in the wake of successful attacks

- By the end of 2021, cyber-attacks are projected to cause $6 trillion in damages

- 91% of small business don't have cyber liability insurance[1]

The data does not lie. It is no longer a matter of IF your business will be hacked, it is WHEN. The amount of risk in the hands of small business owners today is nothing short of staggering. You are not safe and clinging to the old school and lazy strategies of most IT providers will not only not make you unsafe, but they will increase your risk.

Hackers love an easy target. Long gone are the days of installing the free antivirus program that came with your PC and thinking you're protected. The cybersecurity model is broken. Only by adopting a comprehensive and proactive approach can you put yourself in a position to protect your business, and, more importantly, recover when a security event occurs.

Where Cybersecurity Went Wrong

In past, cybersecurity wasn't proactive even though it attempted to be. As soon as new attacks were observed, that attack would be added to a registry of known threats. Various antivirus products would draw on that registry to identify and block incoming attacks at the perimeter of enterprise IT. The only reason this worked to the level it did was that these

---

[1]https://www.fundera.com/resources/small-business-cyber-security-statistics

attacks were infrequent, and most carried with them a sort of signature that could be tracked. Brand-new attacks could still get through, but their effect was short-lived as the antivirus product stopped the vast majority of these attacks.

The above approach worked reasonably well for years, up until about a decade ago. Think of this: In 2009, US cybersecurity spending totaled $27.4 billion. By 2018, that number had skyrocketed to $66 billion and continues to increase exponentially.

So, what happened? Cybercriminals started to create tools that allowed new types of attacks. These tools caused the number of signatures files to explode. Antivirus makers could not effectively keep up with this explosion in new methods. This success by cybercriminals led to a steep rise in fileless attacks and in-memory exploits that would further elude the virus protection of the day. These attacks don't use the signatures that traditional antivirus look for and execute ever-changing behaviors to disguise themselves and bypass gatekeepers without making their presence known.

The response to this is where the problem gets worse. Concluding that they couldn't effectively stop these attacks on the outside, security providers shifted their focus to finding threats hiding on the inside – a fundamentally reactive approach. The results were spotty at best. The new modern attacks are particularly hard to spot or stop because they leave few traces within the vast and growing amount of data that modern security solutions need to collect and process. It's similar to spotting a needle in a haystack.

This new shift has caused companies to spend billions of dollars on detection and mitigation over the past decade, investing in newer technologies like behavioral and heuristic analysis promising to uncover the tracks of these fileless and in-memory threats. Undeniably, the reactive approach to cybersecurity that still dominates today has been an utter failure.

Changing the Narrative with Proactive Cyber Defense

Businesses settled for a reactive approach because they assumed it was the only option. The flaws in this strategy were painfully obvious as any meaningful alternative was not available. However, that's changing as proactive cyber defense is becoming the dominant strategy. Instead of seeing the perimeter as inevitably vulnerable, companies are starting to move their emphasis earlier.

Security-savvy companies are closing the gaps that exist in their security through concepts such as hardening, credential control, and security training. These companies see proactive cyber defense isn't just a possibility, but a priority in a time when a single successful attack can bring a company to its knees.

The idea that companies can stay in front of cybercriminals and hackers, outrunning their attacks as opposed to absorbing the blow, challenges the narrative surrounding cybersecurity. With the right policies, technologies, and philosophies in place, attacks can be prevented, including the most dangerous fileless and in-memory variants.

Taking a proactive and comprehensive approach creates an unbroken defensive perimeter around the business. With that said, any attempt at proactive cyber defense foils many attacks because they're not used to encountering resistance before reaching their objective. Years of reactive cyber defenses have made hackers complacent and somewhat lazy. By finally removing the obvious weaknesses and gaping holes in a security perimeter, proactive cyber defense meets hackers at the point of attack and short-circuits their attacks before they have any real negative effects.

Why is Proactive Cybersecurity Better?

A proactive approach to cybersecurity includes preemptively identifying security weaknesses and adding processes to identify threats before they occur. Adversely, a reactive approach involves responding to incidents as hacks and data breaches, at best, as they are occurring. Tasks involved in reactive cybersecurity are primarily focused on rectifying immediate incidents and preventing repeat attacks or technology disruptions from happening in the future. Our proactive approach utilizes tasks that allow your business to identify and prevent incidents from ever becoming a threat.

There are obvious benefits of a proactive cybersecurity strategy. Most importantly, cyber threats are becoming more complex and smarter, so more than ever before, businesses need to stay ahead of these threats before they can damage your organization.

A proactive approach helps define a baseline level of cybersecurity consisting of the necessary starting point at which software, processes, and professionals are needed to protect your business. With this baseline established, reporting and responding to potential threats can be automated so that your IT service provider will be immediately notified and take action in real-time.

Additionally, not having an effective, proactive strategy in place as the value of data and information continues to grow can cost your business dearly. For example, there are harsher regulatory penalties being levied for not properly securing data as politicians and regulators crackdown on companies that don't adequately attempt to secure their data.

Establishing a Proactive Cyber Defense

Transitioning from reactive to proactive cybersecurity involves incremental enhancements to your existing strategy. Ensuring that key features, which we'll discuss later, are in place is only part of the overall process. Although a major step, implementing the individual features without an overall strategy still will not cut it. The first thing that we require all of our current and prospective clients is to do a full cyber risk assessment.

Understanding Your Risk

A cyber risk assessment is about understanding, controlling, and mitigating risks created by and through technology across your organization. As businesses rely more on information technology and information systems to do business, the inherent risks continually increase. Risk, as defined by The National Institute of Standards and Technology (NIST), is the likelihood of reputational or financial loss. NIST also establishes the three factors that feed into a risk vulnerability assessment. They are:

1.   What is the threat?

2.   How vulnerable is the system?

3. What is the reputational or financial damage if no longer available or breached?

What this does is give us the risk equation: Risk = Threat x Vulnerability x Asset Value. Unfortunately, this is a very simplified formulaic analogy. Calculating risk is not nearly this straightforward, much to everyone's dismay.

Today's IT firms, whether they like it or not, are risk management firms. We employ a variety of tools to help us identify a business's risks that allow us to put in place the tools needed to mitigate those risks.

The primary purpose of a cyber risk assessment is to help inform decision-makers and support the proper risk responses. They also provide an executive summary to help executives and directors make informed decisions about the security of their organization.

In addition to those mentioned, there are several reasons you would want to have a cyber risk assessment performed regularly. Let's discuss just a few:

- Better organizational knowledge: When you know what vulnerabilities are within your organization, you are better equipped to make decisions on where your organization needs to improve.

- Avoid data breaches: This is self-explanatory; data breaches can have a huge financial and reputational impact on your business.

- Avoid regulatory issues: There are serious consequences for those businesses whose customer data is stolen because you failed to comply with regulations like HIPAA or PCI DSS.

- Data loss: How would your business survive if data such as trade secrets, software code, or other key informational assets were stolen, and your competitors ultimately ended up with them?

- Avoid downtime: All systems, both internal and customer-facing, need to be available and functioning properly for staff and clients to do their jobs.

- Reducing long-term costs: By identifying potential threats and vulnerabilities and then working to mitigate them has the potential to prevent or reduce security incidents which ultimately saves your business money and/or reputational damage in the long-term.

We can spend multiple chapters on the importance of and the parts of a solid cyber assessment, so I'll sum it up with this: A cyber risk assessment is vitally important to your business and it should be treated as such. If your current IT provider or department isn't doing them now, ask them why or reach out to a company like mine, PC Dynamix, to have a full assessment performed.

Systems and Tools to Mitigate Your Risk

Now that you have an idea of where your risk lies, you can have systems, policies, and practices put in place to help reduce your risk. While every business can be different, all must analyze controls that are currently in place and determine if they are the best controls moving forward. Are the controls in place to minimize or eliminate the probability of a threat or vulnerability or to react when a breach or anomaly has been detected? Controls should, therefore, be classified as a preventative or detective control where preventative controls attempt to stop attacks and detective controls try to discover when an attack has occurred.

I know what you're thinking: OK, I get it. Now, what should I do? Here are some systems and features that should push you down the path to a proactive cyber defense approach.

Security awareness training

As stated earlier, human error still accounts for more than half of all data security breaches. In many cases, that's not the end user's fault. What some business owners and users consider common sense, many users don't give a second thought. With a proper security awareness training program, you can teach organizations, employees, and families how not to get hacked, which makes them the first line of defense against today's increasingly sophisticated cybercriminals. Today's security awareness training programs are quite good. Most are served to end-users as three to four-minute videos that are made to be engaging and entertaining. The service that we use in our security offering bases every video or episode on a real company that suffered a significant breach, so learning is based on real-world occurrences. It's important, however, when choosing a platform, to make sure there is not an over-focus on one particular attack vector and that users are not overwhelmed with technical terms and jargon.

Multi-factor authentication

Multi-factor authentication is important, as it makes stealing your information harder for the average criminal. The less enticing your data, the more likely that thieves will choose someone else to target. Most everyone is using some form of multi-factor authentication now, especially in the banking and financial industries. Multi-factor authentication, or MFA, is a technique that requires a user to present at least two factors that prove their identity. For example, when you use your online banking app, you'll need to enter your username and system password. Instead of logging into your bank information, the app now sends a text message to a pre-determined number that needs to be entered in before you can access sensitive information. While cell phones and keycards are currently commonplace, this technology is expanding to include fingerprints, iris scans, and other types of biometric data. Adding this secondary factor to your username/password greatly increases the protection of your privacy.

Threat hunting

Threat hunting is the practice of proactively searching for cyber threats that are lurking undetected in a network. Cyber threat hunting digs deep to find malicious actors in your environment that have slipped past your initial endpoint security defenses. Threat hunters assume that adversaries are already in the system, and they initiate an investigation to find unusual behavior that may indicate the presence of malicious activity. Threat hunting is highly complementary to the standard process of incident detection, response, and remediation. As security technologies analyze the raw data to generate alerts, threat hunting is working in parallel – using queries and automation – to extract hunting leads out of the same data.

Email Filtering

The average small business received 94% of its detected malware by email. A 10-person company receives, on average,

90 email-borne malware threats per month. Email filtering stops the junk and lets the good email through. Messages containing offensive, harmful, or policy-violating content are held for user review, while good messages continue on their way. Email filtering helps keeps users safe and gives you confidence that your email infrastructure is shielded from harm.

Zero-Trust Policies

Zero-trust approaches allow businesses to take complete control over what software is running and block everything else, including ransomware, viruses, and other malicious software. This introduces concepts such as:

- Application Whitelisting - Set policies to automatically block untrusted software from running, whether executed by a user or an exploit.

- Ringfencing - Control how applications can interact with each other, and protect network resources, registry, and your data from misbehaving software.

- Storage Control - Control what devices, applications, and users can access individual storage devices and how they access them.

- Detailed Audit Files & Application Access - Audit all file and application access in real-time, for both remote and local users.

- Enforce Encryption - Comply with HIPAA, Sarbanes Oxley, and other compliance requirements by enforcing encryption of portable storage devices.

Backups, Backups, and more Backups

It is amazing that in this day and age clients still need to be reminded of the importance of properly functioning backups. Backups need to be automated and stored on both local and online means. Access to the backups should be protected with multi-factor authentication and the data needs to be fully encrypted. Cybercriminals are becoming more and more sophisticated and are including common backup vectors in their attacks. With that, it is also no longer good enough to just be collecting backups. The backups, both data, and system, should go through periodic and regular recovery tests to make sure important systems and data can be recovered quickly and accurately in the case of a breach or down event.

Dark web monitoring

The dark web is a part of the internet that isn't indexed by search engines. You've no doubt heard talk of the "dark web" as a hotbed of criminal activity — and it is. You can buy credit card numbers, all manner of drugs, guns, counterfeit money, stolen subscription credentials, hacked Netflix accounts, and software that helps you break into other people's computers. Dark web monitoring brings peace of mind knowing you are proactively protecting your company's brand, employees, executives, and customers.

Managed security operations center

A managed security operations center (SOC) centralizes the essential monitoring and incident response functions to a team of experts that can best protect your company's data assets. At PC Dynamix, we provide this capability as a key part of our cybersecurity platform. We provide a managed service that detects malicious and suspicious activity across three critical attack vectors: endpoint, network, and cloud. The service includes an elite team of security veterans and experts who proactively hunt and investigate threat activity across your entire network.

On-going cybersecurity risk assessments and vulnerability scanning: I know we covered this already, but I can't stress the importance of it enough. You review your insurance coverage with your agent at least once per year. You have regular checkups with your doctor and/or dentist to ensure your health and prevent future problems. Your car has regular maintenance performed to keep it running safely and at optimum performance. Your business technology is no different! The only way to keep your business as secure as possible is to make sure you are regularly examining what is at stake and where your vulnerabilities lie.

In conclusion, businesses of all sizes need to become and remain vigilant when addressing the growing and evolving security threats across the business landscape. The outdated, reactive approach to cybersecurity is no longer acceptable. Businesses must evolve with the threats and proactively take steps to ensure safety, efficiency, and longevity.

Moving to a proactive cybersecurity model is challenging and extremely involved. You shouldn't do it alone. Consult an experienced IT provider that has a security first model. Whomever you choose should be able to provide your company with the methodology and policies for building a proactive cybersecurity culture throughout your business. Also, remember that this is not a one-time issue to address. Your cybersecurity protection is a living, growing thing that needs nurturing, tweaking, and refining that is on-going. With a solid, proactive cybersecurity approach, you can make sure the business has a long, profitable, and secure future.

About the Author

George McCracken is the Co-Founder and President of PC Dynamix, a Managed IT Services firm, and Co-Founder and President of MPX Cyber, a Managed Security Services Provider. Mr. McCracken has over 25 years of experience in the IT and technology industry. Before founding his current companies, Mr. McCracken supported and managed teams that supported some of the most high-tech companies in the world, including Intel, Samsung, Micron, and IBM. George's roles have included providing front-line support and managing both technical teams and projects to achieve top performance in one of the most competitive industries in the world.

As President of PC Dynamix, Mr. McCracken has built an agile and award-winning IT services provider. With clients ranging from small and medium-sized businesses to schools and educational institutions, Mr. McCracken provides his clients with a vast depth of business knowledge across multiple industries.

PC Dynamix is focused on providing the very best IT & cybersecurity services while forming a bond and partnership with its clients. In addition, George has laid the foundation of PC Dynamix "People-Friendly" service delivery and continually strives to make technology an asset for PC Dynamix clients and not a problem. With that goal realized, George will now be focusing on providing cybersecurity-focused services through the newly formed MPX Cyber. This new venture will provide businesses throughout the US and the world services to protect themselves through today's ever-changing security landscape.

If your business is struggling with cybersecurity or IT concerns, Mr. McCracken is available to speak with you. To book a short introductory call with George, go to http://1x1withgeorge.com or visit our company websites at http://www.pcdynamix.com and http://www.mpxcyber.com.

Inside the Mind of a Hacker

By Amir Sachs

We tend to think of hackers as determined demons, hunched over a keyboard in a dark room. Green light glaring from their glasses, desk filled with cans of Mountain Dew or other high-caffeine beverages, as they try again and again to break into a system.

Well, that might have been true a long time ago, but today's hacker can be a teenager in a hoodie, using an off-the-shelf hacking application they purchased online. And as for putting in hours of effort, hackers—from *script kiddies* to veterans—now make use of automated systems that simply scan networks looking for weak points to attack. Once detected, the attacks can also be automated, with results sent back either for re-sale or as an open door for more pressing attacks.

What all of these hackers have in common is a lack of moral compass—to the point of sociopathy. Whether they are in for the thrill of the hunt or engage in financial crimes or industrial espionage, they all seem to have a cold heart and no regard for the extreme harm they leave in their wake. Indeed, many appear to take pride and joy in the destruction they leave behind.

Originally, hackers were intellectuals exploring this new realm of computer software. At MIT, for example, the mechanical engineering students proudly called themselves *gearheads*, while the electrical engineering students called themselves *hackers*. There are still plenty of good hackers around. Called *white hat* hackers, they turn their intelligence, curiosity, and deep knowledge toward discovering software vulnerabilities before they are discovered by the bad guys and exploited. White hat hackers are public servants, alerting companies to holes in their software (or hardware) products—albeit with the enforcement threat of *Fix this now, or we will tell the world.*

This isn't to say that criminal hackers and other *bad actors* (a term often used to describe hackers employed by governments) aren't intelligent. They are, but it is an intelligence gone wrong. And, truth be told, today's hackers don't need to be nearly as intelligent as they once were simply because of the terrible wealth of hacking products that can be purchased online. (Do an online search for "hacking tools" and you'll get *millions* of hits.) Many hacking products even provide help desks.

Yes, Even Your Small Business Can Be Attacked

In my work at Blue Light IT, all too often I hear a small to medium-sized business owner say something to the effect of: "Who would want to break into our system?" This might have been a legitimate point several years ago, but today the answer is: "An automated hacking system that has no idea of who you are but can detect a weak spot and automatically execute an attack against that vulnerability."

Hackers, in fact, love small and medium-sized businesses because they are more likely to lack the dedicated 24x7 security teams that keep software updated and continually monitor for intrusions. According to a report[2] from the Beazley Group, 62% of ransomware attacks are done against small and medium-sized businesses.

And the attacks can be devastating. Sometimes clients will come to us after the fact. After all of their data has been rendered useless by an encrypting ransomware attack, or after all of their customers have received infected spam e-mails from them. And they are devastated to hear that in many cases it is simply too late. When you lose access to all of your data, unless you have a robust backup and data recovery plan already in force, you may actually lose your entire business.

Please Do These Two Things . . . *Now*

The remainder of this chapter looks at how hackers get inside, and what they do once they're in. And more importantly, I'll provide 10 steps on how to protect your IT resources from attacks. But first, I would like to make two suggestions that could save the life of your business:

1) Hire a computer security consultant to analyze your existing infrastructure to identify and remedy vulnerabilities that might be attacked. These could include out of date operating systems, applications, drivers, and other software missing the latest security updates and security patches. Unless you have a world-

---

[2] https://www.beazley.com/Documents/2020/beazley-breach-briefing-2020.pdf

class security team monitoring your systems 24x7, you should enter into an ongoing relationship with a security consultant to ensure your systems are always running the latest versions—with all security patches applied.

2) Have this security consultant create a robust, multi-pronged backup and disaster recovery system— including cloud-based and other off-site, off-network, solutions. And make sure it is regularly validated. In my work I've seen systems that have been completely frozen by a ransomware encryption attack—only to have to tell clients (who arrive after the attack) that their backups were stored on the same network that was attacked, and are therefore also encrypted.

The beauty in taking these two actions is that hackers— automated or actual—are looking for the easy way in—the unpatched operating systems and applications. It's like locking your car at night. A prowler will just continue looking for an unlocked vehicle. Secondly, with a robust backup and disaster recovery system in place, even if you are attacked and your data is frozen, you can ignore ransom demands. You are already set to get up and running again. You might lose a few hours—maybe even a day or so—but you won't lose your entire business.

How Hackers Get Inside

As already noted, hackers look for weak spots in your IT infrastructure. Vulnerabilities can give hackers (again, real or automated) access through your e-mail accounts, firewalls, remote access, browsers, applications, connected devices, and a spectrum of other software points that haven't been updated to plug known points of entry.

Hackers also make use of social engineering attacks—sending e-mails asking recipients to click on a link or inserting pop-up windows masquerading as legitimate operating system or application messages, asking the user to click to install an update—which is actually malicious code. Such attacks are referred to as *phishing*. A more sophisticated form, called *spear phishing*, involves crafting messages designed to appeal to specific employees. HR employees, for example, might be invited to a non-existent local dinner or asked to apply for a new position. Whatever the story, the aim is the same: Click here . . . and the malicious code is uploaded. Yet another version, called *vishing*, involves a phone call: "This is Amazon security. Someone in another state used your account to purchase an iPhone. Was that authorized? No? Here, download this code so we can fix the problem. And . . . so we can send you a refund, please give us your checking account information."

Or someone calls and claims to be from your internal IT team: "We need to update an application. Here's the remote desktop app we need you to download so we can get into your system remotely to fix it." Yikes! The examples go on and on and on.

What Hackers Can Do Once Inside

Once inside, hackers and other bad actors can create mayhem in myriad ways. Remember, inside the mind of a hacker, there is joy in breaking in, and completely no remorse for the damage they cause. Here are just a few examples of what they can do once inside your network:

- **Capture and Exploit Your Contacts**. Hackers can break into your system to download copies of all of your contacts, using automated software. Once they have automatically downloaded your contacts, there is a black market for this data. Reputational damage can follow if your contacts are targeted with *phishing* e-mails that appear to come from you, making it more likely they will click and become infected. Not a great way to tighten your bond with customers and colleagues.

- **Go from Phishing to Spear Phishing to Whaling**. Hackers and other bad actors can also use your contacts, and e-mail files, to learn your organizational structure to launch more precisely targeted *spear-phishing* attacks . . . including *whaling*, which refers to targeting CEOs and other big targets. A whaling attack might take the form of an e-mail, seeming to come from the CEO, asking the CFO to wire large funds to a fictional party.

- **Use Your Platform for Illegal Operations**. The nightmare scenario here is to have a SWAT team appear with a battering ram to knock down your front door and hold your family at gunpoint as they confiscate every computer in the house and handcuff you because one of your computers has been (unknowingly) used to download and sell child pornography. Compromised computers can also be joined into a network of other compromised computers, sometimes called a zombie network to generate spam, search for systems to attack, or carry out other malicious activities.

- **Conduct Industrial Espionage**. Bad actors, often working for hostile governments, can use phishing and other vectors to implant malicious code to embed an advanced persistent attack (APT). An APT involves gaining long-term, undetected access to a network in order to explore data systems to locate and siphon off the intellectual property and other high-value data.

- **Launch a Ransomware Attack**. Recent years have seen a long line of companies, healthcare systems, schools, and other organizations being attacked by ransomware. It is a bad way to make the news. And the incidence is increasing. Ransomware is one of the fastest-growing crimes online, because it is so lucrative to criminals, and so hard to trace because of the common demand of ransom payment in bitcoin, which makes transactions untraceable.

10 Steps to Protecting Your IT Resources

I get joy and satisfaction from my career in providing organizations with tighter security for their IT resources. It feels great to engage with a client and be able to discover and remediate vulnerabilities before they can be exploited. Of course, each engagement is different, and each infrastructure unique, but from my experience, here are 10 steps I'd like to share to help you protect your IT resources:

1) **Strictly Adhere to System Updates and Security Patches**. Yes, I mentioned this above. But that is because it is so enormously important. Hackers look for unlocked doors and open windows. They have tools that scan the Internet searching for systems with known vulnerabilities—that haven't been updated or

patched. And, as noted above, if you don't have a top security team working 24X7, you need to engage with a security consultant long-term, because there is nothing static about the threats to your cybersecurity. The attacks are relentless, and continually evolving. You need someone with deep security knowledge on your side.

2) **Continually Scan for Intrusions**. You need to continually scan your IT resources for intrusions and the presence of malicious software. If a hacker gets access to your system today, they may not launch the attack straight away. There is often a delay of two to three months or more from the time you are breached, to the delivery of ransomware. Why? Because they take their time identifying weaknesses and planning for the most opportune time to attack. Constant monitoring can help you identify the presence of unauthorized remote desktop protocol (RDP) configurations, unexpected software, the creation of phony administrative accounts, or the disabling of your security tools.

3) **Maintain a Robust Backup and Disaster Recovery**. As mentioned earlier, a strong backup and disaster recovery system can turn an otherwise devastating attack into a bump in the road. The key is to have a bullet-proof system. In addition to backing up data—to multiple secured locations—it should also include image-level backups that capture the complete current state of your data, and the supporting operating systems and applications. This means that if you need to restore from backup, all of your operating systems and applications will be current and fully patched and

configured. This system should also be tested regularly. Backing up is the essential first step. But you must also ensure that you can restore from it. The need to test the ability to restore comes from experience. I've seen users, for example, who have backed up accounting applications, only to later find that the backup didn't include the actual data.

4) **Deploy Anti-Ransomware Software**. Some good news is that several publishers have created solid anti-ransomware software. There is always an arms race going on, but anti-ransomware software locks down access for typical resources required by ransomware and watches for unusual behaviors associated with it. Remember that hackers and other bad actors are usually searching for easy targets. Good anti-ransomware software helps get you off that list.

5) **Hide Your Passwords**. It's bad enough to get your e-mail hacked and contacts stolen, but another threat is that hackers can search your e-mail, or other folders, searching for the passwords you use to access network resources, and beyond—such as for your online banking. We had one client who thought he had come up with a convenient way to store all of his passwords. He created a contact named "Password" and filled the notes section with all of his account names and passwords. Fortunately, he deployed a new solution before this could be exploited. Here's a quick test you can do right now: Search your Inbox and other folders for "password" or "pass." Whatever you find, is what a hacker would, too. Take advantage of safe password storage applications or create your own store with a

name that has nothing to do with passwords. And . . . for goodness sake, don't re-use passwords for multiple accounts, or use the same naming pattern. Remember, the longer and more complex, the more difficult it is to hack using dictionary attacks and other methods.

6) **Protect Your Contacts with 2-Factor Authentication**. We are all dependent upon others protecting access to the contact information they store on their computers. An efficient way of accomplishing this is through the use of two-factor authentication. The slight downside is that whenever you log into your email from a new device, you need to confirm that it's you by entering six digits from a text message typically sent to your smartphone. But the upside is immense. Even if someone learns your password, they won't be able to access your account because they won't be the one to receive the authentication code.

7) **Don't Be the Easy Target … We Can Hide You**. Returning to the analogy of the car prowler, hackers are looking for unlocked doors. If you work for a big-name organization, hackers and other bad actors may make concerted attempts to crack into your system. But for the typical small to medium-sized business, if your door is locked, if a dog barks, they will just continue to the next target. We can lock your doors; we can make a dog bark (intrusion detection) and we can make you invisible on the network, so they won't even see your front door. Of course, all of this points back to the first step in this list: Strictly Adhere to System Updates and Security Patches. That's how you lock the door, and the windows, too.

8) **Disguise Your Guest Wi-Fi**. If your business is called Acme Anvils, don't name your Wi-Fi guest account Acme Anvils Guest. You don't want to advertise this doorway into your network. Choose a random string of alpha-numerics or employ other strategies to disguise the account.

9) **Encrypt Your Data**. A great way to protect your data is to encrypt your data. If a hacker breaks into your files and finds nothing but encrypted data, they have found nothing of value. Ideally, data should be encrypted while being sent to others (including server-to-server) and encrypted while stored. One downside is that there can be a slight delay in processing, as encrypted data must be decrypted prior to use, but depending on what you are protecting the benefits can be enormous. If you don't want to encrypt everything, you might start with HR files and financial documents. Please Note: Encrypting your data *won't* protect you against a ransomware attack. Ransomware simply re-encrypts your encrypted data, making it useless.

10) **Educate, Educate, Educate Against Social Engineering and Other Threats**. I've written a lot about phishing, spear phishing, whaling, and vishing, simply because they have proven to be so effective in getting users to click on links that download malicious code, including ransomware and the APTs of espionage. (And I could have mentioned *smishing*, which uses text messages (SMS+phishing) to trick recipients into triggering the download of malicious code.) So, education is essential. Not just one-time training, but continual updates on the

dangers, and the new forms hackers and other bad actors have created to trick users into action.

Security is an enormous field, of immense global importance. There is much more to say, but I feel confident that following the 10 steps above, while not definitive, will at least help you get onto a more secure foundation. Wishing you all the best. Stay safe. Stay secure.

About the Author

Amir Sachs is an Information Technology Executive with 25+ years of experience in the SME market across multiple industry sectors. He is appointed as a trusted vCIO, CTO and CISO for multiple companies, both in the US and internationally. In 2003, Amir founded Blue Light IT, based out of Boca Raton, Florida, where he and his team provide IT management, Cyber Security services and strategic technology direction for companies of all sizes. Having worked in the IT industry at a time when the internet started, Amir was exposed to the onslaught of hacking attempts from the beginning, and as a result has gained inside knowledge as to how hackers think and operate. This knowledge is implemented in all solutions provided by Blue Light IT.

Prior to founding Blue Light IT, Amir owned and managed various businesses including manu-facturing, distribution, retail, hospitality, and Import/Export. The experience gained in these businesses gives Amir the ability to quickly understand the myriad of challenges his clients experience and enables his firm to provide technology-based solutions.

Amir's favorite quote is "Impossible, it's only a level of difficulty."

Amir is available for speaking engagement and consulting. Contact Amir on:

LinkedIn https://www.linkedin.com/in/amirsachs

Facebook https://fb.com/mspbocaraton

The Importance of Email Security

By Fred Hughes

Imagine being an accounting clerk or a CFO and you receive an email from the CEO asking you to send a wire transfer. It's a normal occurrence for the CEO to ask you to send wire transfers, because you do it all the time, and this email looks no different. It's not an outrageous amount of money; it seems normal compared to the other ones that you've sent, so you send it. Your heart sinks when you find out it wasn't really your CEO that sent that email and you have to tell him you just sent $18,000 to a scammer.

A friend of mine referred me to a potential client, and when I met with them, they told me that story. It really happened. And, truthfully, it happens quite often. The FBI's Internet Crime Complaint Center (IC3) estimated in their 2019 Internet Crime Report $3.5 Billion in reported losses.[3] The IC3 also stated:

"The most financially costly complaints involved **business email compromise**, romance or confidence fraud, and spoofing, or mimicking the account of a person or vendor known to the victim to gather personal or financial information."[4]

---

[3] 2019_IC3Report.pdf

[4] https://www.fbi.gov/news/stories/2019-internet-crime-report-released-021120

Cybercriminals are getting so sophisticated in their methods of attack that it's getting much harder to tell the difference between what is real and what is fake. What can be done to safeguard the average email user?

THE HISTORY OF EMAIL

First, let's talk about how it all started. There is a longer history than I want to go into here, but the first computer mail messages were just files that were placed in folders. When other users opened the folders, they could read the messages. But those messages were on the same computer. In 1969, the US Department of Defense oversaw a project that interconnected four university computers for the first time. This project was known as ARPANET (**A**dvanced **R**esearch **P**roject **A**gency **Net**work) and was the early stages of the internet as we know it today.

In 1971, Ray Tomlinson, a computer engineer for MIT, developed a system for sending messages between computers. He was the person that initiated the use of the at-sign (@) to separate different usernames and machines. Anything before the @ was the username, and the name after the @ represented the machine name where the other user was located. Tomlinson placed two computers next to each other and sent the first-ever electronic mail message (email) from one computer to another.

Unfortunately, it wasn't long after that, in 1978, when the first spam email was sent by Gary Thuerk, the marketing manager of Digital Equipment Corporation (DEC). Why do we always have to ruin a good thing!? At that time, there were only 2600 users of the ARPANET and he sent his marketing email to 400 of them promoting the new DEC computer, which generated

$13 million in revenue. And you ask does spam work? Judge for yourself.

YOU'VE GOT MAIL!

Remember those AOL disks? You would see them everywhere, from boxes of cereal to airplane trays to boxes of steaks! They gave people a free trial of dial-up internet access that came with an *aol.com* email address. People could get on the internet, and also send and receive email. The Moviefone-sounding voice "You've got mail!" became very popular. AOL also had chat rooms people could participate in, which could be considered a precursor to the social media platforms we have today... communicating with other people around the world while not knowing who they are.

So how many people use email? As of March 2020, the number of global email users amounted to 3.9 billion and growing.[5] Since we know many people have multiple email accounts, do we think 50% of the world population uses email? Many people have both a personal and work email address. Either way, that's a lot of email addresses and a lot of emails. *Statista* states that roughly 306.4 billion emails were sent and received each day in 2020.[6]

HOW IT WORKS

How does email work? If you use email, as far as you know, you open your email editor of choice, type in the email address of the recipient, compose your message, and hit send! Easy right? What does that look like under the hood?

---

[5] https://www.statista.com/statistics/255080/number-of-e-mail-users-worldwide

[6] https://www.statista.com/statistics/456500/daily-number-of-e-mails-worldwide

In the early days, before the Graphical User Interface (GUI), computer commands were executed on a command line, in plain text. First, the user would have to make a connection to the mail server they wanted to send to, then they announced who they were, who on that server they were sending to, and then what the message was. Then they would send the message, then quit, or drop the connection. Sounds simple right? And that's what it was called, Simple Mail Transfer Protocol, or **SMTP**. It is an interactive session, however, with the remote server responding to the commands to acknowledge that it received them.

Here is an example:

S: 220 smtp.server.com Simple Mail Transfer Service Ready

C: HELO client.example.com

S: 250 Hello client.example.com

C: MAIL FROM:<joe@acme.com>

S: 250 OK

C: RCPT TO:<bob@mail.com>

S: 250 OK

C: DATA

S: 354 Send message content; end with <CRLF>.<CRLF>

C: <The message data (body text, subject, e-mail header, attachments, etc) is sent>

C: .

S: 250 OK, message accepted for delivery: queued as 12345

C: QUIT

S: 221 Bye

In the example above, an e-mail message is sent from **joe@acme.com** to **bob@mail.com**. The sender's e-mail address is specified by the MAIL FROM command and the recipient's e-mail address is specified by the RCPT TO command. The DATA command informs the server that now the message data will be sent (e-mail header, body text, etc.). The single dot below the message contents informs the SMTP server when the message data ends. After a single dot has been sent to the server and the server has responded, a QUIT command is sent to terminate the session.

In modern times, that same thing is happening, but with an easier-to-use interface for the end-user. For example, if you're using Microsoft Outlook or Outlook Online or Gmail, you just fill in a form to send your email. You fill in the recipient's email address, a subject, and your message. You can even include things like a signature or images or your company logo. You can also include links, for example, to social media sites or websites. To send your message, just click the send button.

Using our example from above, what if someone were to enter the MAIL FROM command, and instead of putting *their* email address, they put in *your* email address, and then sent a spam email or a malicious email to hundreds, thousands, or even millions of recipients? At one point in time, it was that easy for the shady characters to impersonate someone else like this. It's called an open mail relay.

Junk Mail, Ugh!

So why would someone want to impersonate someone else just to send a bunch of SPAM emails? For starters, sending

SPAM email is illegal now. In December 2003, President George W Bush signed into law the *Controlling the Assault of Non-Solicited Pornography And Marketing (CAN-SPAM) Act* of 2003 and required that the Federal Trade Commission enforce the provisions of the Act. These are some of the fraudulent practices that are viewed as criminal offenses:

- Sending multiple spam emails with the use of a hijacked computer

- Sending multiple emails through Internet Protocol addresses that the sender represents falsely as being his/her property

- Trying to disguise the source of the email and to deceive recipients regarding the origins of the emails, by routing them through other computers

- Sending multiple spam emails via multiple mailings with falsified information in the header

- Using various email accounts obtained by falsifying account registration information, to send multiple spam emails[7]

With current security measures employed by all email service providers, large amounts of spam being sent from a single account or a single IP address would be quickly shut down, so the attacker might not get very far. But if he can compromise someone else's account and send out as many messages as he can before it gets shut down, and just repeat that over and over, he can get a larger number of messages out to the masses.

---

[7] https://en.wikipedia.org/wiki/CAN-SPAM_Act_of_2003

WHY ALL THE SPAM?

What types of messages get sent? There are some email messages that we would consider junk mail. Just like those flyers, coupons, and postcards you get in your real mailbox at your house, people are trying to sell you something. But maybe you signed up for something on purpose. Maybe you visited an online store, and the pop-up enticed you to sign up for their email specials and receive 20% off your first order. So, you fill it out, confirm it (so they know it's a valid email address), place your order, get the discount... but now you're on their list. Their emails come in regularly and you either delete them or leave them in your inbox, unread. Oftentimes you just leave it because one day you might want to go search for it and see if the deal is still available when you need it. But the company sending you that email can track it. They know if you opened it. They know if you opened it *and* clicked on a link inside, and *which* link. If it was for a special offer that ends on Friday, and here it is Thursday night, and you never opened it, a good marketing company will send you another one automatically saying something like, "Hey we know you are busy, but we think you might have missed our email about the special that ends *tomorrow.*" They want to entice you to open it, click the link, and take advantage of the offer, or register, or whatever it was they wanted you to take action on. Guess how much it cost them to send that message vs sending that actual postcard in the mail? Not much. Whereas AOL spent over $300 million on those CD's they sent to everyone in the mail (and everywhere else).[8]

---

[8] https://techreport.com/news/20171/aol-spent-over-300-million-on-those-trial-cds

VIRUSES, MALWARE, PHISHING AND MORE

Just like the junk mail you receive at home that probably goes straight from the mailbox to the trash can, so does your junk *email* likely go straight to the junk mail folder or deleted items folder. It becomes a habit for you. Most spam filtering programs even do this automatically for you and you end up not even seeing much of it anymore.

Because of this, not only do spammers need to be more creative to have their messages make it to your precious Inbox, hackers and other nefarious characters are also becoming more and more creative in their methods to get their messages into that Inbox. But they aren't necessarily looking for you to *buy* something from them. No, they're looking to *take* something from you. Whether it is your data, your identity, your customer records, credit card information, it could be any number of things that will be of value to them, or to someone they can sell it to on the dark web. More than 3.8 million records are stolen each year in cybercrimes and by next year the cost of a single data breach will exceed $150 million. [9]

Malicious software, or **Malware**, is more of a catch-all term for any type of software with malicious intent. A virus is a specific type of malware that can replicate and insert itself into other programs. A computer virus is similar in function to a human virus: it can spread by attaching itself to legitimate files or programs and then can be distributed through infected flash drives, websites, and emails to other computers. If the virus or malware can be installed on the computer, it can replicate very

---

[9] https://www.policearrests.com/resources/combating-cyber-crime-statis-tics/#:~:text=By%20next%20year%20the%20cost%20of%20a%20single,cybercrimes.%20How%20to%20Protect%20Yourself%20Against%20Cyber%20Attacks

quickly across a network as it will have any network access that the user has.

Ransomware is one of the worst types of Malware, in that, just as the name implies, it will infect your computer and hold you for ransom. This malicious software encrypts all of the files on your computer, and some can even infect connected USB and network drives, rendering the computers useless until the ransom is paid. The attacker will usually set a time limit by which the ransom must be paid in bitcoin. By using bitcoin, the payment is final, untraceable, and cannot be canceled. If your only backup was a USB drive, it will have been encrypted as well. Thieves typically give the user the key to unlocking their files, because if word got out that they weren't providing the unlock keys after payment, no one would pay the ransom. But you cannot be sure you will get the key, and even if you do, you cannot be sure all of your files will be recovered properly. It is estimated that the monetary loss from cybercrime has reached over *$1 trillion*.[10]

Phishing is the term used when an attacker is attempting to lure you with their bait, to click on a link, or to open a file. They craft emails that look like they are from someone you know or trust. Some very real-looking emails look just like they're from Microsoft or Amazon. At the time of this writing, the world was experiencing a global pandemic, and at certain times in some locations, people were quarantined or confined to their homes under mandatory lockdown. With these types of restrictions in place, many people turned to delivery services like Amazon, GrubHub, and DoorDash to get food and other necessary items delivered directly to their door. People were used to receiving

---

[10] https://www.mcafee.com/enterprise/en-us/assets/reports/rp-hidden-costs-of-cybercrime.pdf

email messages with confirmations or tracking information, so for an attacker to create an email that looks like it's from Amazon saying click here for tracking info, you can only imagine how many people wouldn't think twice and just click the link. They even send **Vishing** (voice-phishing) or **Smishing** (SMS/Text phishing) messages, expanding their options to attack their prey. You receive a text, looks like it's from Amazon, says "Delivery Delayed, click here for more info." People don't think twice about clicking and they are taken to a site that says sign in to confirm your identity; they sign in, but they are on the attacker's website. The attacker collects the person's credentials, then pass them through to the real site and the user is none the wiser.

HOW CAN YOU BE PROTECTED?

You will find plenty of examples throughout this book describing protection as layers and layers of protection. That, and education. Education is key because there will always be someone, somewhere that finds a way around all the protection and gets inside. It's like those action movies where the hero has to fight through all the henchmen to get to the villain, then they stop, and they look each other down, and then the final battle ensues. In the end, the user can be left staring down the villain, albeit an invisible one. But I cannot stress enough how important it is to put all the layers of protection in place *in front of* the user, to hopefully prevent them from having to engage in that battle. Furthermore, in the event something gets through, there is a safety net if something does happen.

Email Security, a layered approach

It all starts with your email account. Let's face it, we all hate changing our passwords all the time. We have so many now. But here's how most people treat their passwords:

- 73 percent of online accounts use duplicated passwords

- More than half of consumers (54 percent) use five or fewer passwords across their entire online life, while 22 percent use just three or fewer

- Almost half (47 percent) of consumers rely on a password that hasn't been changed for five years[11]

Think about it: if a hacker broke into your Netflix account, well, they will get to watch a lot of free movies. But if they broke into your email account, they can do a lot of damage. As I mentioned earlier, they can use your account to send more of their attacks, posing as you until your account gets shut down. They can also use it in another way. Most of your online accounts use your email address as the username. By reading your emails they can find out where you bank, and if you have Paypal or Venmo or any other types of accounts that can send money. They just go to that login screen, choose *forgot password*, and when they get the reset link, they reset it and log in. They change your email password so you can't get back in, they change your bank password so you can't get in and they start draining your accounts.

Multi-Factor Authentication

One way to stop that is with Multi-Factor Authentication. **(MFA)** By using MFA, you not only have to enter your

---

[11] https://www.telesign.com/resource/telesign-consumer-account-security-report

username and password, but you also have to enter a one-time password from some other method. It can be an app on your mobile device, it can be a text message to your phone. I prefer the app since the hacker could very easily change your phone number in the account to his and he would receive the text message. It's harder to do that with MFA. Several people in our neighborhood have security cameras and are posting the Ring app or Nextdoor app showing someone late at night going from driveway to driveway checking car door handles. Which one does he break into? The one that wasn't locked!

Dark Web Monitoring

The Dark Web is where compromised email addresses go to be sold. If your email address and password were compromised in a large data breach, hackers have access to it. Depending on what it has access to, it can go for pennies or up to $1,000 apiece. Using a service to monitor the dark web for your corporate domain will alert you if a company email address shows up on the dark web. Unfortunately, you can't do anything about that. In the case of another company's breach, it wasn't your fault. But armed with the knowledge that it happened, you can be sure to change that password... and the password of *any* other site you used the same password. (Which is a no, no, by the way. Don't do that either!)

Enterprise Email Security and Filtering

While many of the big providers are getting better at filtering spam and viruses, their primary focus is to make sure your mail gets delivered. Third-party email security providers focus on security. It's important to have email security in place that can monitor all inbound and outbound email traffic in real-time and provide filtering of spam and viruses and added features like URL Defense. URL Defense is when the links in an email get re-written to redirect the user through a website where the security provider checks the site first to make sure it is safe, and if it is, redirects the user on to the site. This all happens instantaneously. All of the major email security providers are now using some form of Artificial Intelligence (**AI**) to help combat the onslaught threats.

DNS Filtering

Remember the thief walking down the street checking door handles? It's great that almost all of the doors were locked, but what is an additional security measure? Park the car in the garage! Now he doesn't even have a door to check. Your email domain, the part that comes after the at sign (@) designates who you are. DNS, or Domain Name System, is the backbone of the internet. Every server in the world has to ask some other server where a particular address is. The information is exchanged and propagated all around the world. Even though we've pretty much dropped the "www" when going to websites, it's usually still there but has an alias that says, eh, we know what you mean, you want this address. For mail, there is an MX record or Mail Exchanger record. Remember the SMTP commands earlier? When you send a message, the mail server looks up the numerical address of the server where that domain's email server is housed. It finds it by querying a DNS server and asking for the address associated with the MX record. Some protections have been put in place in recent years to make sure that the address mail is being sent from really matches where it says it is from. With a real letter, you have your return address in the top left corner, and the person you're mailing the letter to in the center. You could drop that in any mailbox in the US, and it would make it to the destination. You could write a fictitious return address in the top left-hand corner and it would still make it to the destination. That is an example of the Open Mail Relay we spoke of earlier.

DNS protection like SPF (Sender Policy Framework), DKIM (Domain Keys Identified Mail), and DMARC (Domain-Based Message Authentication, Reporting & Conformance) are all types of optional information you can attach to your domain that confirms the sender's address before allowing the message to be sent to you. If a bad guy were trying to send from a mail server that was spoofing someone else's domain name, it wouldn't match up with the mail server that is associated with the MX record of that domain, so it would reject it.

Endpoint Protection

This is one step past email protection, but it deserves an honorable mention. If for some reason, an email message was able to pass all the tests mentioned above and make it to the Inbox with a virus attached and the user downloaded the attachment and executed it, strong enterprise-grade endpoint desktop protection should stop, block, prevent, or otherwise rollback any malicious program trying to run.

End-User Training

Besides strong passwords and multi-factor authentication which gives you access to an email account, the second most important thing you must do is get trained. If you work for a company or if you are a small business owner, you must have end-user training for your employees. Training on how to use all the things we've discussed, multi-factor authentication, strong passwords, not reusing passwords, not having the same password for everything, and not just adding a 1, 2, 3, incrementally every time you're forced to change it. And then getting awareness training. There are great training programs available for companies to get their employees trained on how to spot phishing emails, spear-phishing (targeting specific individuals or groups), whaling (targeting senior officials), and other deceptive emails. They can also provide fake phishing exercises where phishing emails are sent on purpose and tracked to see who opened them, who clicked on links inside, and who didn't open them at all.

BACKUP AND CONTINUITY

This is the final piece of the puzzle. We always hear people say to backup your data! But many don't think to back up their data in the cloud, like email and file sync and sharing programs like, OneDrive, Sharepoint, Dropbox, and Google Drive. Most people think, well, it's in Microsoft's cloud, I don't need to back it up, that is my backup. If you read the fine print on these cloud email and storage providers, they state in their terms & conditions that they are not responsible for your data. They could accidentally delete your account, or a mailbox, or some other quirk, and poof, all your email is gone! A cloud backup service can back up your email to another location not on the same servers as your provider, providing you with the data should you need to restore it. Email continuity is when, for example, if there was a brief Microsoft outage, and their email service was down for any length of time, you wouldn't be able to get your mail. With an Email Continuity solution, your mail would be stored at an alternate location until the Microsoft server came back up, and then it would be forwarded to your inbox.

FINAL THOUGHTS

You may have heard someone say, "I don't care how you do it, just make sure it works." Or in the case of email, "I don't care how it works, just make sure I can access it and it's safe." For me, I like to know at least a little bit about how something works so I can more easily spot if something *isn't* working right, or maybe an anomaly of some sort. Something seems a bit off. That's the first step to spotting potential attacks. In an email, a lot of the time the red flag is noticeably bad grammar. If you apply the layered approach of starting outside your organization, by securing DNS records for your domain and dark web monitoring and then requiring all your users to adhere to sound password principles with multi-factor authentication, strong email filtering and security, and most importantly, user awareness training and testing exercises, you will greatly reduce your chances of significant damage due to an email attack. Additionally, if you employ sound backup solutions and backup & restore policies & procedures, and test the backups, you will have a well-rounded security plan for your business.

About the Author

Fred Hughes is the Founder & CEO of Phoenix Technology Solutions LLC, one of the leading IT service companies in the Phoenix area. With over 30 years of experience providing both technical solutions and services to meet challenging business needs, he has the gift of listening to Client challenges and transforming them into technical solutions.

In 1989, Fred started as a lowly Accounts Payable clerk working for an oil company that was the largest distributor of Exxon products in the world. He quickly moved up the ranks to the computer system manager. Learning the system inside and out, he went on to work for the custom software company that developed specialized software for the petroleum industry. This was an opportunity for him to travel all over the United States implementing the custom software in oil companies across the country, working with CEO's, CFO's, and staff on how to best use the software for their company. It was also very valuable training in dealing with all sorts of company cultures. After several IT Director roles at various companies in Arizona, Fred launched Phoenix Technology Solutions in 2017. Phoenix Technology Solutions has been focusing on the cybersecurity aspect in client businesses and helping companies manage their risk when it comes to technology.

Contact Information:

fjhughes@phxtechsol.com
linkedin.com/in/fred-hughes
https://phxtechsol.com
602-461-7219

Company Name: Phoenix Technology Solutions LLC

Resources: https://phxtechsol.com/resources

For a free dark web scan, text Dark Web to 480 376 1550

You Are A Target: Why Hackers Are Looking For You

By Christopher Bartosz

There is a common misconception among business owners that they do not have anything of value to steal so they would not get hacked. This of course is not the case. Think about your business for a minute. What do you have that hackers want? Data. Hackers want your data. You may be thinking that you do not have any valuable data that hackers would want. Think about your business again and what kind of information you collect from your clients. Do you collect their name, address, phone numbers, email address, or payment information? All of this data is valuable to hackers and they are on the hunt for it every day. The reality is that businesses in every market and of every size are a target for hackers. Let us take a deep dive into the following case study.

What if This Was You?

Imagine coming into the office on Monday morning after a relaxing weekend and seeing a message on your computer screen with a count down timer. The message says your files are encrypted and will be permanently lost if you do not pay the ransom. You perform a quick search in My Documents and see that your files are encrypted. After the initial shock wears off, you are left with two options. Pay the ransom and hope the hackers give you back access to your data or restore it from backup. You have a disaster plan in place with a backup of your critical files, so you start down that path. You quickly realize there is a problem when you check your backups and nothing is there. How can that be? You get startled by the phone ringing. On the line is a very angry sounding client demanding why you are requesting access to their bank account? Confused, you assure the client everything is OK and advise them not to fill out the form as it was some kind of mistake. As soon as you hang up, the phone starts ringing again. Your biggest client is on the phone, screaming at you for spamming all of their employees and crippling their email system.

This case study is a classic case of what is going on in the world today. Years ago, hackers would break into your system and encrypt your files. You would pay the requested fees and eventually get your data back. Today hackers are breaking into your systems and hiding out for days or weeks before you even realize they are there. In the background, they change your backups to only backup meaningless files, so you have no choice but to pay. Besides, they are downloading a copy of your data, and if you choose not to pay, they go after your clients.

What Motivates Hackers

Hackers have many different motives for their destructive behavior, but it all comes down to money. There are many ways they profit from your business data. One of the most common ways they profit is by selling your data on the dark web. Some hackers just sell your data as-is for a really low price. Other hackers will compile your data with other data they have stolen and create a complete client profile. They clean the data to make sure it is valid. This complete data can be sold for a much higher price. Some hackers even offer a guarantee that the data they are selling is competitive and valid or the buyer gets their money back. The price they get for the data depends on the type and amount of data they are selling. For example, if they are selling just a social security number, they may only get $1 for each unique record. Credit card data may go for as low as $5 with just the credit card number and three-digit security code. If they are selling complete credit card information with name, address, card number, expiration date, security code, and even bank information, that can go for $30 or more per record. The data is not limited to just credit card numbers. Sensitive medical data can be sold for over $1000 per record depending on what is included in the file.

Email addresses are very popular and useful to a hacker. If they steal your client data complete with name and email address, they can use this information to go after your clients. While this data seems to have little value, it enables the hackers to perform targeted phishing attacks on your clients. Since they know you have had some contact with these addresses, they can spoof your email domain and send targeted and personalized messages to your clients. Why would they do this? Simple, they do this to gain more information about your clients. There are two main reasons for this. One reason is the new data they collect can be added to your client's file making it more valuable to sell. The second reason is they can potentially trick your client into giving up passwords or other personal information. Since they are making their email look like it is coming from you the client is more trusting of the email and thus more likely to click on any links in the email and potentially provide sensitive information. An example of this would be requesting a password change to one of your systems or a system the hacker knows your client has access to. Your client then becomes the hacker's next victim. The hackers can now use this information as a launching point to see what other systems your clients have access to. Most people reuse passwords for multiple websites, like their credit cards and online banking.

Recently hackers have changed the way they do business. If you decide not to pay the ransom, they use your data to extort the money from your clients. They do not use the same demand they gave you. They tell your clients that they hacked you and you refused to pay so now they want the money from your clients, or they will release the data to the dark web. This not only exposes your business by telling the world that you were hacked, but now your clients are stuck footing the bill.

Hackers get excited when they find sensitive information on children. Children's information is some of the most valuable out on the market today, especially social security numbers. This is because no one is watching the child's credit file until they turn 18. This can give hackers years to open different lines of credit in the child's name. By the time it is caught, the hackers are long gone. A child's credit file is rarely ever checked. Most adults either have some kind of credit monitoring or at least check their credit report periodically, thus shortening the time some of the data can be useful.

Today all businesses store some kind of data electronically. Without taking proper precautions, the data is vulnerable to attack and theft. While you hear in the news almost every day of some large corporations, school system, or government agency being hacked, you don't always hear about the small businesses. Statistics show that nearly 60 percent of small to medium businesses that get hacked go out of business within six months. Why is that? First, you have the damage to your reputation with clients and prospects. Clients want to know that you are doing everything possible to keep their data safe and if you get hacked, they lose that trust in your business. The second is the cost of recovery. Even if you pay the ransom it can still take days or weeks to recover all of the data. Backups are great, but restoring an entire business takes time. This loss of productivity and ability to serve your client affects the overall health of your business.

While this all sounds scary and hopeless, it is not. You can protect your business if you take the proper precautions. With the ever-changing cybersecurity landscape, no solution can be purchased, set up, and forgotten. You do not put gas in your car once and think you never have to fill the tank again. You not only fill the gas tank frequently, but you also check the oil, keep the tires full, and use gauges to monitor the engine. The same applies to your cybersecurity. You have to monitor and test your security solutions regularly. After you get hacked is not the time to find out it is not working. The days of thinking you are not a target for hackers are long gone. Every business is a target. Every business has something a hacker wants.

What You Can Do

There are some common security solutions you should have in place to protect yourself from hackers.

First, you should have a hardware firewall. The equipment you receive from your Internet provider does not have the full capabilities of protecting your network and reporting on events. The hardware firewall is your first line of defense in many attacks. Having the ability to report and monitor network activity in real-time allows your IT provider to block suspicious activity.

Second, you should have advanced endpoint security solutions installed on every computer on your network. The days of using a "free" anti-virus or purchasing a yearly license are over. Advanced solutions are a multitude of security solutions, there is no one solution to rule them all. Each product has a specific purpose and monitors different types of activity. All of these solutions need to be constantly monitored and fine-tuned to make sure they are protecting you from the latest threats out there.

Third, have a solid set of security policies and procedures and making sure you and your employees are following them. The policies outline what is acceptable behavior for using the business's computer systems.

Fourth is continued education and testing. This goes along with having policies in place. You need to monitor and test employees to make sure they are following all of the recommended procedures. Continuing education sounds time-consuming, but we can keep employees trained and up to date with the latest threats in short weekly or monthly videos. Since hackers are always changing how they attack, the training has to constantly change and happen to keep everyone in the know of what they need to look for.

Finally, the mindset. You need to adopt a security-first mindset. Having all of the protections in place but not following your own procedures or having a qualified IT company monitoring your solutions is like leaving the door open to your house so hackers can just walk in and steal your stuff. We provide our clients with a full 360-degree view of their security on a monthly or quarterly basis and make adjustments when needed. We also constantly test the backup systems and train employees through mock phishing and continuing education.

So, are you prepared to answer the most important question: Are you protected, or will you be the next victim?

About the Author

Christopher Bartosz is the President and CEO of FVC Technologies based out of Chicago, IL. FVC Technologies focuses on servicing small to midsized businesses in Chicagoland and across the nation as their outsourced IT department by providing IT management and cyber security solutions. Together with the business owners, Christopher works to develop a technology plan that will grow and change with the company. The plans focus on keeping the company secure and implementing innovative technologies to improve efficiency within the organization. He has extensive knowledge of multiple government regulations that he uses to ensure his clients who hold government contracts remain compliant and secure.

Christopher believes that people should never stop learning. He participates in frequent continuing education to stay up to date on technology and security solutions. He is also a Microsoft partner and can transform your workplace productivity by introducing you to the new Microsoft ecosystem through the implementation of a customized SharePoint solution for your business. He also provides education and security training to the companies he serves.

When not working with other business owners, Christopher unwinds by spending time with his wife Kelly and their dogs. Together they enjoy travelling to unfamiliar places and exploring local cuisine. Christopher also enjoys staying fit by golfing or running and has completed the Chicago Marathon, although his favorite race is the 5k.

Christopher Bartosz

https://www.linkedin.com/in/christopher-bartosz-fvctech

www.fvctechnologies.com

Are You Being Hacked? What to Look Out For

By Izak Oosthuizen

HACKERS - RELENTLESS AND UNSTOPPABLE

Cybercriminals, relentless and unstoppable, want your data at any cost. Malicious PC hacks are getting more advanced and sophisticated every day, so much so that we can no longer rely on technology to alert us of an impending attack. A recent hacking event was so cleverly engineered that it took more than 9 months for it to be identified. 9 months!

Cybercrime is big business and is only going to get bigger.

"Cybercrime to cost the world $10.5 trillion Annually By 2025 - this is a 150% increase compared to 2015."[12]

With the threat of businesses having to pay up billions, and with no guarantee that their data will be safe and secure, we all need to work together to stop cybercrime in its tracks. Here is an example of an 'act of war' cyberattack – the so-called

---

[12] https://cybersecurityventures.com/cybercrime-damages-6-trillion-by-2021
https://www.csoonline.com/article/3110467/cybercrime-damages-expected-to-cost-the-world-6-trillion-by-2021.html

cyber equivalent of Pearl Harbour. Find out what you can do so that you don't fall prey to cybercrime.

18,000 COMPANIES HACKED

In March 2020, IT employees of approximately 18,000 companies using SolarWinds systems and network management software applied an update for the Orion platform. Besides providing network-monitoring and other advance technical services to US government agencies, SolarWinds has hundreds of thousands of global clients, including most Fortune 500 companies. Nobody knew that the new version was riddled with malicious malware that would enable hackers to infiltrate the highest levels of government systems in the United States.

How did this hack, known as Sunburst, occur? Once hackers had penetrated SolarWinds, the rest was easy. They were able to secretly insert the malware into a standard security update, a pop-up that looked identical to all the other updates provided by the IT management software. The hack, known as a "Supply Chain Attack," enabled hackers to surreptitiously send commands through a backdoor, enabling them to do more damage, such as progressive privilege escalation, credential theft, and data theft. The attackers, cunning to the last, used rotating internet addresses and virtual private servers with internet addresses in the target's home country to make detection of the traffic almost impossible to detect.

OVER 9 MONTHS!

Then, a few days after Sunburst, SolarWinds fell victim again, this time to the Supernova hack, installing a backdoor in the same network software. While the Sunburst attack was attributed to Russia, the Supernova cyber-espionage campaign was the work of a different adversary. It was thought that multiple teams were launching parallel attacks.

When and by whom was Supernova discovered? By Microsoft in December 2020 – that's at least 9 months after the deployment of the malware. 9 months during which the hackers had free reign to access the data of US government agencies, defense contractors, and technology providers. The departments of Homeland Security, Justice, Treasury, Commerce, Energy, and State are only a few of the compromised victims.

A security statement from Microsoft posted on 18 December 2020 claimed:

"The investigation of the whole SolarWinds compromise led to the discovery of an additional malware that also affects the SolarWinds Orion product but has been determined to be likely unrelated to this compromise and used by a different threat actor."

SELECTIVE TARGETING

While 18,000 customers applied the update, the hackers only activated their Trojan horse backdoor on a handful of high-value targets. By December 2020, there were only 200 victims. This meant that the hackers, probably part of a national cyber-military team, could be selective and take their pick on who to spy on and what data to steal. For 9 months, they moved from one organization to another, and users were oblivious to the hacking.

THE FIRST DISCOVERY

The first hack, Sunburst, was noticed in mid-December 2020, when the US cybersecurity firm FireEye Inc disclosed that it had itself been a victim of the very kind of cyberattack that clients pay it to prevent. Not good news when IT companies are the victims of cybercrime.

FireEye, who claimed that their problems were 'only the tip of the iceberg,' reported the elaborate intrusion to Microsoft and the FBI. CISA, the US Cybersecurity and Infrastructure Security Agency said:

"Taken together, these observed techniques indicate an adversary who is skilled, stealthy with operational security, and is willing to expend significant resources to maintain a covert presence." [13]

CISA added that once hackers were inside a network, they seemed to focus on gathering information, frequently targeting the emails of IT and security staff to monitor any countermeasures. Such actions accentuate that both Sunburst and Supernova were espionage-driven attacks. [14]

AVERAGE of 280 DAYS

So is 9 months too long? IBM's recent study, the "Costs of Data Breaches Increase Expenses for Businesses Research" shows that it takes an average of 235 days to identify a breach and further 45 days to contain it. If you do the maths, that's a total of 280 days. The table compares the reality of global cybersecurity breaches in 2020 and 2019.

---

[13] https://www.dailymail.co.uk/news/article-9071645/Microsoft-discovers-SECOND-hacking-team-installed-backdoor-SolarWinds-software-March.html
[14] https://www.dailymail.co.uk/news/article-9071645/Microsoft-discovers-SECOND-hacking-team-installed-backdoor-SolarWinds-software-March.html

2020 and 2019 Global Cybersecurity Breach Statistics[15]

	2020 Results	2019 Results
Total cost of a breach	$3.86 Million	$3.9 Million
Time to identify and contain	280 days	279 days
Security automation deployed	59% of organizations	62% of organizations
Costliest industry	Healthcare	Healthcare

WHICH BREACH IS THE MOST DANGEROUS?

It's quicker and easier to contain a breach caused by human error as opposed to one from a malicious attack. Malicious attacks and hackers are stealthy and devious. By design, they want to remain elusive and not get caught. Breaches stemming from employee error are easier to detect since employees are often unaware of the breach and are not trying to conceal it. Although it's faster to contain this type of breach, it doesn't make it any less dangerous. Sending files to the wrong recipients, opening malicious emails, and unwittingly downloading malware could spell disaster for any company. If an employee has wide-reaching access to vital company assets, this could have massive financial and reputation consequences.

---

[15] https://www.ibm.com/security/data-breach

YOU CAN TAKE ACTION

The faster you identify and contain a data breach, the lower the costs. But remember, the hackers of today are quicker and sneakier than ever before. They can compromise sensitive information in the blink of an eye. Put simply, the more barriers and precautions you apply between data and the hacker, the more time you have to identify and deal with threats. There are things you can do. You can act and protect your network, PC, and mobile.

YOUR NETWORK AND PC – WHAT TO LOOK FOR

Messages and Popups

You may get random messages and popups telling you that your device has been infected. These could have a 'Remove Virus' option and clicking this will download malware onto your PC. The message could also contain ransomware and demand money in exchange for your data.

Fake Protection Alerts

Phishers use fake protection alerts to gain access to an administrator's account. For example, fake Office 365 alerts may claim that a license has expired and that users must log in to check payment information. Giving access means that hackers have full admin rights to your network.

Spoofing And Fake Emails

Spoofing emails are fake communications that appear to come from a known source, such as a bank or an online retailer. You are usually asked to reply by disclosing an account number.

Spoof emails can contain Trojans and other viruses, meaning that your data is at risk of compromise.

Unwanted Toolbars

Hackers find ways of delivering malware by installing unwanted toolbars, the most well-known and notorious of these being Ask. These toolbars also slow down browsers, collect search terms, and install adware.

Unknown Software

Unknown software can easily be installed on your machine by clicking on a suspicious link or downloading unknown files. This software is used for phishing, installing trojans, and activating malware. To avoid and remove unknown software, compare what's on your system with your software inventory immediately.

Redirected Internet Searches

Hackers use malicious redirects to force a site visitor to another site. The intention is usually to generate advertising impressions. Malicious redirects can exploit vulnerabilities and install malware on your device.

Social Media Invitations

A typical symptom of social media hacking is when your friends receive invites or messages that you never sent. Large-scale hacks through social media invitations can result in big data loss and identify theft.

Passwords Invalid

A sure sign of hacking is when your online passwords don't work. Hackers typically use social engineering, key-stroke logging tools, and network analysers to crack passwords, access accounts and change passwords.

Online Accounts Exhibiting Unusual Activity

If a hacker has access to your online accounts you will notice unusual activity, anything from social media to various lifestyle or productivity applications. This hacking could reveal itself by activity on your accounts, such as resetting a password, sending emails, marking unread emails that you do not remember reading, or signing up for new accounts when verification emails are in your inbox.

Spam Emails from Company Email Accounts

When you suddenly start receiving complaints that spam emails are coming from you, it might be a sign that you've been hacked. On an individual level, regularly check the sent items for messages that you don't remember sending or look like spam. Losing control over your emails will have a negative impact on your organisation's reputation and will also turn off off a prospective customer.

Missing Money

Do you see unusual transfers out of your bank account? Your PC might have been compromised or it could have been from you responding to a fake phishing email from your bank. The hacker can then log into your account, change your contact information, and transfer large sums of money to themselves or another party. They would often transfer to a foreign exchange location or bank. Always monitor your bank accounts.

File Access Denied

If you are unable to access your files it is very likely that your pc has been infected with ransomware. Ransomware normally will start encrypting all your files and is downloaded from attachments to phishing emails or via an installation from an infected website.

Slow Systems Access

General slow access to systems might be the result of a hack; this normally happens when multiple systems flood your bandwidth or systems resources. Many breaches are first identified by unusual, unanticipated network traffic patterns. These types of attacks are also known as a denial-of-service (DDoS) attack.

Confidential Data Leaked

Nothing confirms that you've been hacked more than when your confidential data has been revealed out on the dark web or internet. Data leaks normally occur via compromised PC's, emails, or USB keys.

Moving Mouse

This method is not as common as some other forms of cyberattacks. Hackers will break into a PC, wait for it to be unused for a long time, and then try to take your money. Hackers can break into bank accounts and transfer money, even trade your stocks, and carry out many rogue activities.

ON YOUR MOBILE – WHAT TO LOOK FOR

Mystery Pop-ups Alerts

Constant pop-up alerts could indicate that your mobile has been infected with a form of malware that forces devices to view certain pages. This could also be a form of Adware that collects revenue. That doesn't always indicate a complete compromise, but may also have phishing links to try and get you to share sensitive information or download other more dangerous malware.

Random Changes You Did Make

Malware can also be hidden and make changes to your configuration settings, home screen, or set bookmarks to suspicious websites.

Any configuration changes you didn't make indicates a hack!

Slow Performance

Your mobile frequently freezing, or some applications crashing, or you find that applications continue to run, despite your efforts to close them. This can be a sign of malware that is overloading your mobile's resources.

High Data Usage

Unusually high data bill at the end of the month, which can come from malware in the background sending information to rogue servers.

Random Calls or Texts You Didn't Send

If you're seeing lists of calls or texts to numbers you don't know, you have been hacked. These might even be premium-rate numbers contacted by malware. Always monitor your mobile bill.

Decrease in Battery Life

Any mobile that has been compromised will display a significantly decreased battery lifespan. Malware may be using your mobile's resources in background, constantly scanning your mobile and sending the information back to rogue servers.

Linked Accounts Exhibiting Unusual Activity

If a hacker has access to your mobile, they likely have access to your online accounts. You will notice unusual activity, anything from location verification popups to social media notifications, to various lifestyle or productivity applications. This hacking could reveal itself by activity on your accounts, such as resetting a password, sending emails, marking unread emails that you do not remember reading, or signing up for new accounts when verification emails in your inbox.

CRITICAL CHECKS

Besides applying best practises and recom-mendations around cybersecurity, we need to be more and more vigilant with our approach. We need to do everything to proactively identify anything suspicious.

We need to modernise our approach by ensuring we carry out these critical checks and implementing these cybersecurity strategies in the workplace:

Multi-Cloud Security Strategy

Ensure that you apply a multi-cloud security strategy to your systems. Integrating the cloud into your existing enterprise security program is not simply adding a few more controls or point solutions. This crucial step in securing your data requires an assessment of your resources and business needs to develop a fresh approach to your cybersecurity culture and cloud security strategy. To manage a cohesive hybrid, multi-cloud security program, you need to establish visibility and control. Many security products and experts can help you integrate appropriate controls, orchestrate workload deployment and establish effective threat management.

Breach Response Plan

A data breach response plan is a strategy put in place to combat breaches after they occur to diminish their impact. A well thought out plan ensures that every person in a company knows their role during a breach to discover, respond, and contain it promptly. These plans provide peace of mind during a crisis since the steps are already tested and specified, as opposed to formulating a plan during a breach.

Use the Right Tools

By automating your security you will be able to contain a breach proactively and more quickly. Firewalls, network assessment tools and antivirus are no longer enough. You need to have every single point of your system monitored and protected, including your staff. These tools can no longer only be technical but they need to be practical. Train your staff – get them on an automated security awareness program, monitors their progress and schedules phishing campaigns to give them real-world tests!

DO NOT GIVE UP

You don't need to become a victim of cybercrime like SolarWinds and FireEye. You might think that these 'grave' threats, intrusions that remain undetected for a long time, are impossible to prevent. They are preventable and you can do it – just don't give up.

By being on guard, alert and implementing best cybersecurity practice, you can stop the damage in its tracks. Protect your network, PCs and mobiles – that's the only way to stay cyber-safe. Also, do not be fooled into thinking hackers only target corporations. Hackers love small businesses (SMBs) as they are often less secure, easy to penetrate, and a platform through which bigger companies can be invaded. Reflect on these closing words:

"More than half of all cyberattacks are committed against small-to-midsized businesses (SMBs), and 60% of them go out of business within six months of falling victim to a data breach or hack."[16]
"Cybercrime is probably the biggest challenge that humanity will face in the next 20 years"[17]

Yet again, don't give up! There are many things that we can all do to bring down hackers and end the expensive misery brought on by cybercrime.

---

[16] https://cybersecurityventures.com/hackerpocalypse-cybercrime-report-2016
[17] https://cybersecurityventures.com/annual-cybercrime-report-2020

About the Author

Izak Oosthuizen has over 20+ years of experience in numerous IT functions from an operational perspective with a strong focus on risk mitigation and cybersecurity. He has worked and collaborated with the likes of UK Space Agency, WeWork, Energy UK, Edmond De Rothschild, Federation of Master Builders, and Dimension Data.

Zhero is a Microsoft Gold partner providing tailored risk mitigation, cybersecurity, cloud, business IT support, consultancy, and professional services to a range of industry sectors including finance, legal, insurance, architecture, and advertising.

Izak pioneered the "Zhero Cloud", a practical, secure, and all-in-one solution for SME's, available for a fraction of the costs compared to other public offerings. As part of the "Zhero

Cloud" solution customers in architecture, video, and advertising get a unique, fast serverless system.

Izak is also a member of the Entrepreneurs Organisation London and has a passion to help people experience the transformative power of IT. He has a ground-breaking 99% client retention over the past 10 years.

Are you concerned about security? Book a strategy call with Izak here:

https://calendly.com/izakoosthuizen/30

Understanding the Risk of a Cyber Attack

By Ron Trotto

It is not a matter of if your business will be subject to a cyber-attack. It is only a matter of when. Not all cyber-attacks result in a breach, but it is critical to understand the risks involved if your company becomes a victim of a breach. Once cyber-risks are determined, stakeholders can make informed decisions around what we will call a "risk appetite." A business's risk appetite is how much risk a company can withstand and still be viable. A cash and carry retail shop has an entirely different risk appetite versus a medical office versus a public accountant versus a government subcontractor. In some businesses and for some industries, mandatory compliance drives low risk appetites. Let's look at some examples of the most relevant risk factors for small businesses resulting from a cyberattack.

The "Can you do me a favor?" email

Typically, this email goes out to a direct report to a C-level employee or owner. The email goes something like this:

"I am traveling/with XYZ client, and I want to give them some gift cards to show our appreciation for having the meeting. Please run out and get me some XYZ gift cards, grab the numbers and the codes from the back so I can give them to

them today. We really need this account. Please take care of this now. "

In a small business, this one typically does not work, but you would be surprised how many of the 20-100+ employee companies fall victim to this one.

The "Need to wire transfer" spear-phishing email

This email is targeted very much like the preceding example, but it usually goes to the finance person, and it looks like it is coming from their boss or manager. The exchange is typically fast and furious and ends up in a wire transfer request. Again, you would be surprised how often this is successful. Seeing this come through and dealing with companies that have fallen for it in the past, I can tell you that the bad actors are brilliant in that the stories have all been plausible and timely. They are expert level, social engineers.

Let's look at another example by running through a scenario on this one. You own a manufacturing company with direct sales. After a long holiday weekend, you log into your computer, and you are prompted with a popup that says you have been ransomed. You knew this day was coming, and after a long holiday weekend, you are rested and ready to enact that plan you had in place with your IT provider, and away it goes. Everything works according to plan. While you are down for most of the day, you do not have to meet the ransom demands, which are 10% of your annual revenue. Your best estimate is that you have lost a half-day of productivity from your staff, and web orders were halted for a half-day, so you have a 25% loss of daily order revenue as half of the people who could not place an order return. Everything is back up and the business is up and operational. You have already considered a business interruption and you are confident that your insurance company will cover most of the losses if you made a claim.

Now, let's take that scenario and shift it to a Friday during your busiest season. While the restore goes swimmingly as in the first scenario, there is a gap in backups, so you have lost a day's worth of orders in the system during your busiest season in addition to the time you are down restoring from backups. You have to bring people in on the weekend to fill the demands to keep delivery promises. As you can see, a single day in a slightly different scenario dramatically raises the risk and financial loss.

Now let's take this example to an extreme. Same as the last scenario, but when you come in on Saturday, you have a message from the bad actor that reads:

"Congratulations on your recovery! Unfortunately, we have been in your system for a while now, and we have all the designs and supplier's information and financial information for all of your products. We will share this with the public if you do not pay three times the original ransom demand. I have attached some pictures of the schematics of your number one selling product to verify that we have this information. You should have just paid the ransom."

This latter example is, unfortunately, becoming the new norm as exposing data is typically more costly to many businesses than encrypting it. In this scenario, what happens if the data is exposed? What if they also reveal confidential design information that one of your suppliers holds a patent on? What if the bad actors can also get everyone's credit card information from the ordering system? What is the cost there?

Financial Loss

As you can see from a handful of examples, there is a considerable risk of financial loss resulting from a cyberattack. In 2019, the average monetary cost of a small business breach was over two hundred thousand dollars. Let's look at this in terms of a more concise list of where financial losses originate.

- **Direct Loss** – We saw this in the first couple of examples. Direct loss is typically fraud directly against the company or employees, resulting in an immediate loss such as the purchase of gift cards or wire transfer.

- **Indirect Loss** – These are the losses associated with the breach, such as loss of income, opportunity costs, etc. In the example above, there was a loss of at least a day of employee productivity and lost orders.

- **Ransom/Extortion** – These are payments made to retrieve information or prevent information from being disseminated. It is important to note that nearly all ransoms and extortions are demanded to be paid with bitcoin. There will be additional costs involved in acquiring bitcoin funds as they are not obtainable from your traditional banking institutions.

- **Remediation costs** - These are the costs that occur as a result of the cyberattack and can be further broken down into:

  - **Cyber Incident Response Team** – These are the professionals that are called in to respond to the cyber incident. This team's cost is typically one of the largest cost components for small businesses while being the best investment for containing the company's overall costs and impact.

- **Cyber Forensics**: The costs to have an insurance-approved third party forensically look at what happened and, in some cases, assist with determining where fortification is needed once systems are restored.

- **System Recovery**: The costs to get your systems back to an operational state. For the examples above, this would include the cost of restoration from backup, creation of new servers, etc.

- **Ongoing Credit Monitoring** – If the data breach includes any critical personally identifiable information (PII), your business may be on the hook to provide credit monitoring to affected parties. Each state has different requirements around response plans concerning exposure of PII.

- **Legal Fees** – The first call small businesses should make at the time of a suspected breach is legal counsel. Suppose counsel is familiar with your company and has been part of the business's incident response training. In that case, there will be significant cost savings and an overall decrease in time of resolution.

- **Lawsuits** – If other companies or individuals are affected by your cyber breach, one will likely get pulled into cases for the individuals and businesses to recover their losses.

- **Fines** – Typically, penalties come with compliance violation and will come as a round-two cost after the breach has happened.

  o **Insurance Exemptions** – These typically fall under the above categories but were believed to be covered by insurance. Small businesses must review all exemptions to ensure insurance coverage.

The review should include a gap analysis by an excellent cyber insurance broker to ensure no surprises when a claim is submitted.

Reputation Loss

The effect that reputation loss has on a company strongly correlates with the company's response as well as the company's line of business. For example, let's take a retail giant with a public breach that exposes credit card information. The company identifies the breach, takes appropriate actions to correct the breach, notifies customers, and offers credit monitoring, although they may not need to. Loss of reputation will likely have a minor short-term effect. By contrast, let's take a bank that prides themselves on their cybersecurity stance, which ends up having a breach which ultimately ends up in financial and loan records exposed to the public domain. This breach is devastating to their reputation even if they go above and beyond. They can likely recover given a prompt and transparent response, though. Now, let's think of the same scenario where the bank was caught hiding the fact considerably after they knew they were breached and chose not to notify anyone. In this scenario, not only will the bank likely not survive, it would be presumed that the top brass would be going to jail.

Regardless of where in the spectrum of those two examples your business might be, it is worth identifying what type of reputation loss your business would encounter over various breach scenarios with your most trusted clients or a representative sampling of such.

Information Loss

In our manufacturing example, what if the bad actors deleted all of the information or they leaked it to the public domain? Without thinking about any of the financial losses, could the company survive this scenario? Take a look at your business and ask yourself, what information do we hold that we cannot survive without? Any intellectual property contained in your systems for your business or other businesses or customers that would be devasting if deleted or maybe worse yet, made public? How about your accounting system? Do you use cloud applications? Is the data in the cloud application critical to your business?

As you can probably gather from the questions above, the first step in identifying information loss risk is identifying where your information is stored. Once you have identified all the areas where you store information, each area should be classified in terms of risk to the business. This classification should not only include risk if the information were deleted, but it should also include risk if this information became available to the public.

As you can see, various potential cyber-risks face small businesses in a cyberattack. The key is to look at each of the risks in terms of impact on your business in the event of loss or exposure to gauge the risk appetite for the company. There is little to no appetite for many compliance-related risks if the company is to remain viable after a significant cyber-attack and breach. Breaches that are found to be non-compliant and are investigated by regulatory entities typically represent a significant financial hit. They also present high-visibility publicly available reputation-wrecking dissemin-ation of breach information as well as the potential loss of certification and jail time if the offense is severe enough.

Anything that needs to be accomplished to meet insurance requirements should also be top of the list. Finding out that your insurance will not cover something based on an exclusion can force doors shut on businesses that end up being victims of a cyber-attack. While we did not directly cover this in determining risk, it should be noted that anywhere that risk is assumed to be covered by insurance should be starred for later review. When looking at the overall cybersecurity plan, review these items to ensure that all insurance requirements are being met.

The concept of cyber-risk has books dedicated to the subject, so we are just barely skimming the surface in this chapter. The key takeaway is that any business that has employees that use an internet connection has cyber-risk. Once cyber-risks have been identified, an appropriate cybersecurity plan can be developed to fit the business's risk appetite.

About the Author

Ron Trotto is the CEO of TC Computer Consulting LLC in northwestern CT. He is a HUGE small business advocate. Coming from a family of small business owners, Ron understood firsthand both the struggle and rewards of owning a business before starting his own business. Although Ron has worked with multiple Fortune 500 companies in his career, he finds working with small businesses to be the most rewarding. He has built his practice around delivering best of class technology services to his clients. His approach lets his clients focus on their core business instead of worrying about its technology, serving as a virtual CTO for most clients. Formally trained as an engineer, Ron has a concrete understanding of systems and was a very early adopter in defining and applying systems in his own business to help other companies manage their technology. As an extension of this structured approach, Ron has always included industry best practices surrounding cybersecurity within his clients' environments for over twenty years.

Ron is a very active member of his local chamber and business councils. He is also a very active member of numerous peer and IT community groups. Ron is a huge fan of the hive mind and readily shares with his peers to strengthen the IT services offering for ALL his fellow small business owners, not just those that are local. Ron is also a vocal advocate of the need for adopting cybersecurity best practices and can be heard and seen translating all the tech babble to plain English, from doing in-person presentations to webinars to social media and authoring books. When he is not in work-mode, Ron enjoys time with family and friends, mentoring a robotics team, or just enjoying the outdoors.

How to Avoid Being a Security Risk

By James Grabatin

It was a sunny Tuesday morning one minute before eight o'clock when Jesse strode into his office at the accounting firm where he worked. The room seemed empty with half of his colleagues working from home and a couple of recent layoffs, but within minutes he would be too deep into his work to notice. He logged into his computer and, as usual, checked his emails first, scanning the inbox for anything urgent to address. He caught a few spammy emails and directed them to the junk folder. After taking care of a request from his manager and responding to a couple of clients, he noticed an email from his bank. "Why did my bank email me? It must be urgent," he thought.

The email stated there was suspicious activity on his account and requested him to review the attachment of the activity. He opened the attachment but was presented with an error window. It was then a red window appeared on his screen. Jesse reached out to Mark, the resident techy staffer. Mark knew what the red notice meant, but he had no idea what to do to stop the nightmare that was to come.

Minutes later, three empty offices away, CEO Barbara sat frozen, staring at the red box on her monitor. She didn't know what to do with the message on her screen. It stated that all her files had been encrypted and demanded a bitcoin ransom. "Where do I get even get bitcoin?" she panicked.

Back in Jesse's office, he felt horrified, then fearful that he was about to be fired. How embarrassing it was to fall for an email phishing scam. What had been put at risk? Employee information? Sensitive client information? His clients worked hard to keep their small businesses afloat, and this year had been hard on some of them. He could not bear the thought of being responsible if they lost their company.

Barbara was angry. Not so much at Jesse – it could have been any one of the team's oversight. No, she was angry about the inconvenience of having to deal with someone's attempt to extort private information and money. They were barely keeping up with all their clients – and now this. If she had been stressed before, this magnified it ten-fold.

Since they did not work with a trusted cybersecurity firm, Barbara wasted many critical hours searching for a firm she could trust. After finally getting some quality advice, she didn't pay the ransom. She was told by paying the ransom she would remain on their hit list for future attacks since she would be a known payment maker.

In the end, Barbara's firm spent two weeks without access to most of their desktops and all their file servers. Months later through a dark web monitoring service, they were informed that some Social Security numbers, personally identifiable information, and client financial information had been breached and were up for sale on the Dark Web. Clients were not happy.

Falling prey to cybercriminals is a business owner's worst nightmare, aware or not. Whether the malicious motives behind these cybercrimes have to do with financial gain, commercial espionage, or political agenda, it hardly seems to matter when everything you have worked for is crumbling around you. Not only do you suffer lost revenue from downtime, but your reputation and trust within the community can suffer when confidential information is exposed.

Fortunately, there are ways you can be proactive in protecting your company from becoming the next victim.

Trust a Professional – Don't play with cybersecurity

Gone are the days when you can depend on the most technologically inclined team member to manage not only your computer maintenance but your network security. It might seem like a way to cut expenses – until the moment something goes wrong. While the tech-inclined team member might dabble in computer-related knowledge, professional cyber security firms spend every single day staying on top of hacker trends and analyzing appropriate security posture. They augment their knowledge by solving similar problems across their client base, not by working in a single environment. The climate of technology is always rapidly changing. What you knew 2 years ago, even 6 months ago, is often no longer relevant today.

Let go of preconceived notions

"It won't happen to me, I'm too small." The infamous last words before the catastrophe. The truth is, small to medium-sized businesses (SMBs) account for 71% of ransomware attacks (Beazley-breach-briefing-2019.pdf). Attackers know

SMBs have been lacking in their cybersecurity posture and target them for this reason. It is time to step up your game.

"I don't need another expense." Cybersecurity can no longer be considered a mere accessory to your business budget and management; it is a necessity. Your entire business relies on technology and, as you have seen in the news, small businesses often shut their doors after a breach. Look at cybersecurity as an investment, not an expense. You have business insurance, right? You should have cybersecurity insurance and a coordinated cybersecurity platform to mitigate not only the financial losses but your reputational loss and the wellbeing of your company and employees.

Get professional support before crisis hits

Having a proper cybersecurity platform in place is a wise way of saving money. The expenditure of a forensic analysis of your entire network is costly and time-consuming. It adds to the stress and lengthens the timeline for recovery. Having a Security Information and Event Management (SIEM) system in place can not only provide proactive mitigation but can vastly reduce the time and effort required in recovery efforts. A Security Operations Center (SOC) can analyze the SIEM data before and during an attack, often minimizing the overall scope of the attack by halting it in its tracks.

Find the right trusted advisor

Find an advisor that follows the Cybersecurity Framework as set by the National Institute of Standards and Technology (NIST). The NIST Cybersecurity Framework is a comprehensive 104 step process that encompasses the entire cycle of cybersecurity. It starts with identifying the assets (both physical and digital), developing a plan to protect those assets, detecting threats, responding to those threats, and complete recovery from a breach. The level of detail in this framework is something you should expect and require from your service provider.

If you're in the financial sector or healthcare, there are regulations you must adhere to protect clients' sensitive data. Look for a partner with knowledge of these compliances. Even if you're not in finance or healthcare, personal information such as names, postal addresses, phone numbers, and even email addresses are now considered Personally Identifiable Information (PII) and need to be protected from exposure. Your IT security partner should know how to find, secure, and track all that data and be able to report on it.

Don't choose ignorance – knowledge is key

Even when you get professional support for your network security, you and your team will need to dedicate yourselves to ongoing education. Hackers do not take time off and they're always looking for better ways into your organization. You need to keep informed as well. Look for a program that not only includes a comprehensive annual certification for all staff but also includes monthly training and weekly up-to-date and relevant tips to keep your team astute.

Know what is at stake

Do you know your complete financial and reputational exposure? What information is vulnerable to exploit, and where exactly is it being stored? These questions can be answered with a comprehensive risk management assessment. This assessment should be performed at least annually and will tell you where your sensitive data lies and how you can protect it. You may discover your sensitive data has been compromised in surprising places.

Perform quarterly cybersecurity reviews

Cybersecurity reviews performed by a competent trusted advisor are an essential way to ensure your company's security posture is where it needs to be. Set it and forget it fixes are not solutions at all. Security tools should be assessed quarterly to ensure they are addressing the current cyber threat landscape.

Protect your weak points

First, be extremely cautious with email. It is a tool we use every day, but it's also the number one entryway into an organization. Be wary of unknown senders. In today's world, a well-coded malicious email can provide an attacker with your email credentials. Ransomware is most often delivered by emails that encourage you to open an infected attachment. And don't believe these emails are easy to spot. Often extensive research is performed on a target to create very believable emails. The more legitimate the email looks, the more likely the recipient is to open the attachment.

Second, perform regular encrypted backups that are stored off-site in a SOC 2 accredited datacenter. Be cognitive of your recovery time objectives (how quickly you can recover) and recovery point objectives (how much data loss you can tolerate) to minimize losses during recovery.

Third, develop and regularly update your incident response plan. Establish an incident response team to work alongside a trusted advisor with the knowledge and capabilities to carry out necessary tasks in the event of a cyber event.

Conclusion

Though cybercriminal activity is on the rise, and hackers have never been busier and more successful, your company can be proactive and avoid being the next easy victim. Do not find yourself paralyzed by fear or overwhelm; begin your search now for a professional you can trust with your network security. Educate yourself and your team on your vulnerabilities and keep up on trending attacks. Secure cyber insurance for your company. Put a plan in place so you and your team know who to call (or better yet, your cybersecurity partner should monitor for attacks and know about it before you do) and what to do when cybercriminals creep past your strongholds. By following these suggestions, you will be able to have peace of mind that you've done your best to protect the relationships and the business you've worked so hard to build.

About the Author

James Grabatin is the founder and CEO of Armor Coded Network & Data Security, located in southern Ontario, Canada. Armor Coded helps the financial sector mitigate cybersecurity risk and delivers high performing IT systems for businesses with 10 to 200 employees. As a natural problem solver, his drive for efficiency and obsession with network security compelled him to specialize his managed IT services in risk mitigation and coordinated cybersecurity platforms. When he is not protecting networks, he can be found enjoying a Cuban cigar or scrolling through cute bunny videos on Instagram with his family.

To educate yourself further on ways to increase your company's cybersecurity posture, download your free security checklist at 15ways.armorcoded.net

The Business Impact of a Breach

By Jerry Swartz

Several months ago, our company Krypto IT Services received a call from a staffing agency because their organization had been hit with ransomware and needed guidance on how to proceed. I explained that if they had not already disconnected the network from the internet, to remove that connection immediately. We arrived at the location and had a meeting with the owners and the IT staff to discuss what had or had not been done. Their internal IT staff had restored a few backups, but the hackers had already reinfected those devices and that is why they had reached out for help with the situation. I asked was the network was still connected they said, "Yes, somehow our mail server was not affected so we left everything going so we would continue to have mail." Well, that's a problem...

We began our work by contacting the Federal Bureau of Investigation Cyber Crime division since a possible 700,000 Social Security Numbers were at risk. They needed to collect data for their investigation before the remediation. We (Krypto IT & their inhouse IT staff) then split into 2 teams. Team 1 was to find the extent of the breach and infection, while Team 2 verified backups for critical systems and began to restore them into the virtual environment to test our temporary network on a separate VLAN after the breach was contained. Before we could bring a temporary environment online, we had to review current security, confer with Team 1 about how the breach occurred, as well as fortify the network, test our security fix, and add a more layered approach to their new cybersecurity defense plan.

Consequence #1 DOWNTIME

Downtime is a common occurrence after your organization has been hit with a Cyber breach (or more commonly referred to as "having been hacked"). A breach's harmful effects disrupt many areas of a business. One of the main issues that organizations must tackle is an unplanned halt in operations, the duration of which is determined by the extent of the breach. How much does it cost to operate your business per day? Woah, this is going to be expensive!

The financial impact to a business after an attack is massive. Some businesses never recover and eventually go bankrupt. The cybercriminals may even be holding the company hostage with malware with the intent to cripple its operations and hold the business at ransom. Some cybercriminals even go as far as posting client information and company secrets to public forums as a punishment for not paying the ransom. Therefore, an effective Cybersecurity plan is always in a company's best interest to minimize the threat vector.

So, do you pay the ransom? That is the question that Dr. William Scalf and Dr. John Bizon had to ask themselves when hackers locked the files at Brookside ENT and Hearing Center in Michigan. The Cybercriminals were demanding $6,500 for the decryption key to regain access to their files. While this was not an outrageous sum, a decision was made between Dr. Scalf and Dr. Bizon to not pay the ransom. Despite hackers having full control over the practice's computer system, there was no guarantee that the files would be restored if the ransom were paid, or that the hackers would not request additional funds following the receipt of the initial request.

Now the business owner calls the Network Admin, IT Manager, IT department, IT guy, or the IT/Cyber Remediation team he hired to triage the damage. Hopefully, they already have an incident Response Plan, Business Continuity Plan, and a Cyber Insurance Policy in place in case of an episode like this. If they have Cyber Liability Insurance, they need to notify their carrier because they might want an investigator to oversee everything that happens so the claim is approved. Even with all these things in place, there will likely be a disruption in the business.

For organizations that lack these critical procedures, depending on the scale of the attack and the amount of data that was affected, it can take weeks if not months for a business to attempt to operate at a normal pace. The average time to identify and contain a data breach, or the "breach lifecycle," was 280 days in 2020. Speed of containment can significantly impact breach costs, which can linger for years after the incident.

Consequence #2 Identify those Affected by the Breach

As backups are restored after Cyber-attack, there remains the human cost, affecting customers, employees, and possibly 3rd party vendors. Assess how severe the data breach was by determining what information was accessed or targeted, such as birthdates, mailing addresses, email addresses, social security numbers, and credit card numbers. This damage can potentially haunt an organization for a long time after the initial attack.

Depending on your state laws and the number of customers affected, you will have to notify all them by a certain period and tell them what you are doing to resolve the issue. At the time of this writing in my home state of Texas, a law was created that as of January 1, 2020, Texas law requires certain businesses that experience a data breach of system security which affects 250 or more Texans has just 60 DAYS from the time the breach has occurred to provide notice of that data breach to the Office of the Texas Attorney General. To comply, you must fill out the Data Breach Notice form provided on their website and submit it electronically. Then the Consumer Protection Division of the Attorney General's office will contact you with follow-up questions if any.

The FTC has a model letter on their website which explains how to notify people whose names and Social Security numbers may have been stolen. It's good practice for these individuals to place a credit freeze with Equifax, Experian, and Trans Union.

Consequence # 3 Damaged Reputation

Once your organization has been hacked it may be a challenge to reverse a damaged reputation. Customer acquisition is costly and it's hard to win back consumer trust. Especially if the user's data affected becomes public record and they now are under attack.

Consequence #4 Compensation Costs

You may have to reassure those affected with some form of compensation such as credit monitoring subscriptions and identity theft insurance policies for a set amount of time.

One example: Equifax—one of the country's three major credit reporting bureaus—announced that criminals had hacked into its computer network. This breach exposed the names, Social Security numbers, birth dates, addresses, and driver's license numbers of around 147 million people. Many lawsuits against Equifax, as well as governmental investigations into the company, followed. On July 22, 2019, Equifax agreed to pay up to $700 million in a settlement over its lapse in security. Much of the money (around $500 million) was earmarked to help consumers.

Consequence #5 Legal Costs

Unfortunately, we live in a litigious society, so lawsuits are routine nowadays. Regardless of whether you win or lose, expenditures can be quite expensive. If the breach happened because your company made mistakes, the right insurance policies may potentially cover some of this.

Regulatory fines are another reality that many businesses overlook. In 2015, for example, the FCC slammed AT&T with a $25 million fine. This was a result of a breach that led to the disclosure of information related to thousands of accounts.

Consequence #6 Government Audits

If your organization is large enough then there is a substantial chance that a government organization such as the Federal Trade Commission (US) will be knocking on your door to carry out an audit. They may even decide to then fine your business if they find that guidelines such as PCI DSS were not followed.

Remember Dr. William Scalf and Dr. John Bizon from earlier in the chapter? Scalf said the attack was not formally reported as a HIPAA breach because an "IT guy" advising them determined the attackers did not view any of the patient records. However, faced with rebuilding their entire practice due to the loss of records, the doctors decided to close their business on April 1 and retire about a year earlier than planned. However, because they had lost access to their patient records, they had no way to communicate closing to their patients. "We didn't even know who had an appointment in order to cancel them." Scalf said, "So, what I did was I sat in the office and saw whoever showed up for the next couple of weeks." After his interactions with patients, it's reported that Scalf worried an investigation would result in charges, so he and Bizon reported the ransomware attack on Brookside ENT to the FBI.

Needless to say, all ransomware attacks should be reported immediately.

Healthcare entities and any entity that faces compliance should find a reputable data forensics specialist to review the files. HIPAA breach notification laws also require that data breaches of unsecured PHI be reported to the Department of Health and Human Services (HHS). The regulation also sets standards for notifying patients that have been affected by a data breach, especially those resulting from a ransomware incident.

Consequence #7   Costs for Remediation

Hopefully, you had a Cyber Insurance Policy in place to mitigate a large portion of these costs. Even with these protections, you may incur losses and possible new taxes based on how the funds were allocated or distributed.

According to the 2020 report from IBM and the Ponemon Institute, the average cost of a data breach in 2020 is down 1.5% since 2019 and cost around $3.58 million USD. This works out to be around $150 per record and is a 10% rise over the last 5 years. The report analyzed recent breaches at more than 500 organizations to spot trends and developments in security risks and best practices.

Another key aspect in this is continuing education to educate employees on proper cyber habits and not to trust e-mail links.

Implementing new software for enterprise-level SPAM filtering, and bringing in a Cybersecurity provider with a CISSP on staff to work with your current staff are also beneficial.

With our growing reliance on the cloud, and the complexity of security systems paired with human error, there are more attack vectors than ever before for criminals to exploit. Just as you would hire an outside accounting firm to do an audit for your business, this practice should also be adopted to audit your in-house IT security to look for any vulnerabilities. This helps your companies help your IT staff to shore up any weaknesses. Having the right tools, people, and processes in place will allow you to detect data breaches early or even prevent a data breach from happening in the first place. Therefore, having files encrypted, a layered security stack, and air-gapped backups are so important. The steadily rising cost associated with data breaches could save an organization millions in the long run.

About the Author

Jerry W. Swartz, CEO Krypto IT Services – Houston, TX

Jerry W. Swartz is the founder of Krypto IT Services LLC, a Cybersecurity & IT Consulting firm based in Houston, Texas. He is an experienced Chief Executive Officer with a demonstrated history of working in the information technology, security, and service industries. Skilled in Customer Relationship Management (CRM), Data Center, Management, Software as a Service (SaaS), Outsourced Project Management and Networking Administration. Through his company, Krypto IT, he and his team of professionals provide a unique blend of scalable, remote IT & cloud-based solutions, resources, and skillsets to address today's threats and future Cybersecurity support needs of businesses & enterprises.

He has been in the technology since 1995 and has been contracted by companies such as United Airlines, EDS, Memorial Hermann, and Texaco to name a few. Their clients consist of Manufacturers, Auto dealerships, Medical Practices, Law Firms, and businesses of all sizes. He is also a heart transplant survivor who goes to the local hospitals to give support and mentor patients who are waiting for transplants such as the left ventricle assist device, LVAD, recipients.

For a free offer go to our site
www.CyberNowBook.KryptoCyberSecurity.com

Cybersecurity Defined

By Whit Taylor

Imagine this! You just got hacked. One of your employees clicked on a link within a phishing email, and now all your computers have been infected with ransomware. You do not want to pay the ransom, but you were not backing up your data properly so you cannot recover it. What do you do?

Well, as mentioned in the previous chapter, if you are the owner of Brookside ENT and Hearing Center, you decide not to pay the ransom, but you pay a heavy price. The hackers delete all your data, including that of your customers, and you end up having to shut your doors and close your business for good.

This is just one of the millions of cybersecurity incidents that have occurred over the years and yet another small business to bite the dust because they did not have the right protections in place. This is a common example of the cybersecurity reality that we face today. We used to be able to be lackadaisical in the protection of our business and data, but we can no longer take that approach. We live in a world where it is no longer a matter of IF we get attacked, but rather a world of WHEN we get attacked. In a world where a hacker strikes every 39 seconds, we can no longer afford to just be reactive to threats. We must take a proactive approach to protect our business and our customers. This is our cyber reality.

So, what does "protecting our business" look like? What does cybersecurity entail? Well, the dictionary defines cybersecurity as the state of being protected against the criminal or unauthorized use of electronic data, or the measures taken to achieve this. It is a process. Like anything worth doing in life, there is a process associated with protecting your business. It is not a fire and forget one-time thing. It is a never-ending journey that must be navigated with a proactive, security-first, mindset.

The cybersecurity threats of our time are ever-changing, with new threats continuously emerging. In 2014, Symantec released a report stating that nearly one million new threats emerged every single day. You read that right. Almost one million new threats emerge each day. Protecting your business is no scenic route drive to Disney World, but rather one of a treacherous hike to the top of Mount Everest. One must be vigilant, or they will face deadly consequences.

Cybersecurity is a difficult and complex journey, but one that is vital for business owners to take. We bear the responsibility not only for our own data and confidential information but for that of our customers as well. No matter what industry you are in, your customers entrust you with some level of personal and confidential information. Those are the stakes. It is not just our reputation and money on the line, but that of our customers as well. That is why cybersecurity is important. That is why we must have a cybersecurity plan. That is why it is so critical that we protect our business.

Cybersecurity is a lot like a jigsaw puzzle. I remember when I was growing up, I was obsessed with putting together jigsaw puzzles. I loved the process of figuring out which pieces went where and even the frustration that came with it, but most of all, I loved the finished work. The masterpiece. What I also remember is the frustration of having a piece or two missing. And a puzzle that's missing a puzzle is worthless. There is no masterpiece with a missing puzzle piece. Just a ridiculous and worthless trinket. Cybersecurity is a puzzle with many pieces. The days are long gone when having a firewall and an anti-virus solution was enough to defend against hackers. We live in a world where the threat to our businesses changes and evolves daily. Therefore, cybersecurity, the protection of our businesses, is much more than having anti-virus installed or having backups. It is a multi-faceted approach that uses many pieces in order to protect your business from cybercriminals and everything they throw at you.

Now, cybersecurity, like all puzzles, requires that you have all the pieces in order to be effective. Just like a puzzle, if you are missing a few pieces, it's essentially worthless. Hackers will find the gaps. They will find the areas that you neglect and at the end of the day, your business will pay the price. They will take advantage of your business. Therefore, it is so crucial to have all the pieces. Cybersecurity is a puzzle, and when you have assembled all the pieces together, you are left with a masterpiece of protection.

That's a simple overview of what cybersecurity is. Now, you may be thinking, "Whit, I have such a small business, there's no danger for me. I'm not a target." I get it. Trust me. I have heard that from more small business owners than you can imagine, and while I wish this was true, the unfortunate truth is that SMB's are a primary target for hackers. The Ponemon Institute reported that two-thirds of SMBs have suffered a cyber-attack in the past 12 months. More than half of all small businesses suffered a cyber-attack. A study also shows that 60% of cyberattacks are against SMB's.

Now, you might think that with that information, SMB's would take measures to close the gaps and protect themselves, but you would be mistaken. It isn't for lack of wanting to, but rather for a lack of people to handle focusing on it. Three out of four SMB's say they don't have the personnel to address IT security, which in turn gets ultimately neglected. I'll address how they can overcome that stat a little later in this chapter.

So, even with this new information, maybe you are still skeptical. Maybe you might be thinking that all those small businesses must have had really juicy secrets and that's why they were hacked. Maybe you think that you don't have anything that the hackers want. Before I dive into this point, I want to tell you a story about someone who had a similar perspective on this. One of my oldest and best clients, whom I shall not name for privacy reasons, did not believe that they had any valuable data, and therefore they were not a target. I went through an entire cybersecurity audit with them, showing them the risk they possessed and the danger they were in, but alas, my warnings fell on deaf ears. They were adamant in their stance that they possessed nothing that hackers desire. They were missing one key piece of information: Hackers don't discriminate.

What do I mean by that? Hackers don't care what information you have. They don't care if it's a credit card number or just an email address. It could be your grandson's baby pictures. They truly could care less. I have seen businesses of all shapes and sizes and of all kinds get taken advantage of by hackers.

Cybercriminals live to take advantage of those who simply are not prepared or who aren't properly protected. And that's what happened to my client. They chose to not protect themselves and about three months later, they suffered a massive data breach. They learned the lesson the hard way. They learned that even though they didn't have "valuable" data, they still were targeted and taken advantage of.

So, your small business is at risk. We've established that, but the stakes are even higher than that. It's not just you at risk. It's not just your business that's at risk. Your clients are at risk. "Okay Whit, now you are talking crazy." I know how it sounds. How could your clients be in danger from your business getting hacked? It's not their business. They don't have to replace broken or compromised equipment. They don't have to pay the ransom. They don't have to pay the fines for possible compliance negligence. It's not their reputation on the line. You're right. None of that applies to them, but they are at risk. What happens if the hackers steal their personal information such as their social security number? Or maybe they steal their credit card number that you have stored for recurring payments? They have entrusted their confidential information to you. The second that they handed it over to you, whether it be a credit card number, ACH information, or other confidential data, it became your responsibility to safeguard that information and protect it against unauthorized access.

So, it's their reputation and neck on the line too. Maybe not as directly as yours, but they are at risk just the same. And they know it too. Not only did they entrust it to you, but when they did, they developed an expectation that you would safeguard it. You may not have told them this, or necessarily agreed to that expectation, but it is the expectation they have, nonetheless. Some may read that and think, "Let them have that expectation. It won't matter for me or my business." A quick word of caution for that line of thinking. If they expect it, and you don't address it, they will sue, and more than likely they will win. So, not only would you be facing the cost of damages, reputation loss, and possible fines due to compliance issues, but you would also be facing multiple lawsuits from angry clients. So, as you can see, the cybersecurity stakes are very high, but believe it or not, they can get even higher depending on your business.

Compliancy is a totally different animal. Depending on the industry you work in, or on the clients you deal with, you may fall under different regulations. You may be familiar with some of the bigger regulations such as HIPAA or PCI-DSS, but there are far too many to list in this chapter. The big thing I want to touch on here is why compliance raises the stakes for you. It's so much bigger than increasing the dollar amount for damages. Let me explain. Imagine that you are the primary owner of a prestigious CPA firm. As with all businesses that handle taxpayer information, you and your firm fall under IRS compliance for safeguarding that information.

If you don't comply, you inevitably will face fines and other financial penalties, but let's dig deeper. Your reputation is tainted now. Not only for suffering a massive breach, but for being a firm that is known for not complying with regulations. Loss of revenue can be overcome with time, but reputations are infinitely more challenging to regain. A study by information-age.com shows that 66% of consumers say they would be unlikely to do business with an organisation that experienced a breach where their financial and sensitive information was stolen. Imagine what that number would increase to if you are exposed as a company that does not heed regulations.

So, what's the moral of the story? Know your regulations and do everything to comply with them. Going back to my prestigious CPA firm example, as an accounting firm, the IRS provides documentation on what their regulations are and do a great job in not only making the details available but also providing guides on how to comply. Not every regulation is going to come with a training wheel per se, but the regulation details are out there for you to seek out and take action.

As you can see, the stakes are very high, and the responsibility falls upon you to ensure that your business takes action. Have you ever heard of Smokey the Bear? Smokey the Bear is a character that is used to illustrate the danger of forest fires. His main talking point is, "Only you can prevent forest fires." Well, the same concept applies to cybersecurity. Only you can prevent a data breach. Cybersecurity starts with you. I know you might be a little skeptical about that statement. I know you aren't a cybersecurity expert, but protecting your business starts with you. It starts with each person within your organization. I'm not saying that your users can stop cyberattacks from happening. No one can truly prevent a cyberattack, but there are things that we as individuals can do that can dramatically decrease the risk of a data breach.

We can practice good cybersecurity hygiene. Just like we shower regularly, floss and brush our teeth, and practice good hygiene in that respect, there are things we can do to have good cybersecurity hygiene. The first thing we can do is be diligent in being safe online. What do I mean by that? Be careful what websites you go to. If it isn't a secure website, you probably shouldn't go to it. The second thing you can do is only work on secure networks. I know we live in a world where Starbucks and other places offer free Wi-Fi, but the reality is that those networks are easy prey for hackers. I'm not saying you can't use them, but I highly suggest that you not access sensitive information while using these non-secure networks. The big thing that we all must do is simply be vigilant. The majority of cyberattacks target our users and ourselves. Human error is the biggest cause of data breaches. Do you know how we prevent that from happening in our businesses? We all must be vigilant.

And while that is nowhere near being the only thing you must do to protect your business, that is where your responsibility ends and where you must rely on a trusted cybersecurity advisor to fill the gaps and partner with you in the protection of your business. Why? Let's just be realistic. As a business owner, you cannot be an expert at everything. Let's take me as an example. As a cybersecurity professional, while I am very well versed in defending against hackers and ransomware, my knowledge is limited when it comes to accounting. That's why I hire an accountant. The same thing goes for why I hire a lawyer or even why any of us hire employees. We can't do it all and we surely can't do the things we aren't experts at.

So that is Cybersecurity defined in a nutshell. I know it may seem like a lot, but if you and your employees are diligent in practicing good cybersecurity hygiene, and if you partner with a trusted cybersecurity provider, you can build that masterpiece of protection I spoke about earlier. It's a process, and like with any process, you must fully commit. You can't go halfway. You must go all in and you can't cut corners. Like I said earlier, a puzzle with missing pieces is virtually worthless. Go all in. Cybersecurity can be a complicated process, but if you tackle it with a security-first mindset, and if you partner with a trusted cybersecurity advisor, your business will be protected, and you will win this cyberwar.

About the Author

Whit Taylor is the Founder and CEO of Unity Cyber, Business Continuity and Cybersecurity Expert, and Information Security & IT Professional. Previously, Whit was the IT Director of a local accounting firm where he oversaw IT Service Management, Business Continuity and Network Security for the accounting firm for many years.

Whit founded Unity Cyber in 2017 to help business owners protect their business assets and confidential data and provide world-class IT services to the businesses he serves. Whit's knowledge and passion about Information Technology and Cybersecurity led him to building a business that helps other businesses continue to grow and prosper.

Whit is a proponent of cybersecurity awareness and takes pride in helping business owners see the true value of security and how to truly protect their business assets and confidential data (that of their clients and their own). Whit is not only extremely knowledgeable in IT and Cybersecurity, but he also focuses on helping businesses attain disaster readiness and implementation of business continuity and solutions that will help business owners prepare for unforeseen disasters that may occur including severe weather, flooding, fires and cyberattacks.

In his personal time, Whit is an advocate of his local church and has a deep passion for helping his community. He spends his personal time with other members of his church, helps out in the kids and youth ministries and is the lead keyboardist in the band.

Connect with Whit on his website: http://1x1.unitycyber.com.

How Human Error Can Cost You Thousands

By Joseph A. Vitti

Imagine being warned over and over again by someone you know and trust that you need to do a certain something to protect you from a certain something else happening to you. Imagine it's something pretty bad or scary. Imagine telling this person, "That will never happen to me!" Imagine it happening! Because this is pretty much how life works, right? It gets you when you least expect it.

Imagine you're this guy named Johnny. You've been running a small family business with 10 employees. It's been in the family for 40 years and you are extremely busy, working in the field all day and trying to catch up on emails and paperwork at night. Your life is crazy. And you've been sure to tell people how busy you are for the last 10 years and have done very little to try and fix it.

Anyhow, it's 10 pm and you're checking up on your emails in the office, Johnny. Go home already, sheesh. You come across this email from your bank that says you had a problem with your account and directs you to download a statement. You are exhausted, but now you are also terrified. You click and take a look. It asks for your email address and password, you put it right in and boom, you got a statement. Oh, wait...

Something pops up asking you to click run in order to view your bank statement. OK! You click it. Moving right on. Let me see my statement already! Right? Not right, Johnny. You never could get that statement to open, and it's late, after all, so you just go home and call it a night. You decide to call the bank in the morning to find out what happened.

You walk into the office the next morning, bright and early of course, and sit at your desk sipping your morning coffee. Wiggling the mouse, your computer wakes up, and you see something strange which you've never seen before. The screen is covered by a message that says "Your data has been encrypted. You have 2 days left to pay and get your data back. After 2 days we delete everything." You're freaking out. Everything was fine yesterday! You ask around the office to see if anyone else is having this weird problem with their computer. Come to find out, every computer in the office has this big red window covering the screen, "2 days to pay."

Well, Johnny, now you're about to blow a gasket. All these people are unable to get any work done. You completely forgot about the bank statement you wanted to look at. You have to call the IT guy, immediately! He can fix anything!

That's when you call me. I start asking you a hundred questions about how this happened and at this point, you can't remember clearly what you were even trying to do on your computer last night. You just need this fixed immediately.

Now, I'm going to give you a little backstory here. You recently hired me to help you out with your IT on an as-needed per-request basis. I never took over any type of management role with your IT systems, and we have no contract. We just pick up the phone when you call and try to help out. You could never get in touch with your old IT guy, so now you call us instead.

I come to your office and take a look. I found out that you had some backups in place. I was able to get rid of the ransomware on your computers, restore your data, and get the company back up and running in 3-4 hours. Not bad. You are happy! You thought this would be so much worse. After all, you've read all about this stuff in the news, but you never thought it would happen to you! Well, anyhow, your IT guy (me) did some magic and saved you, you're all set. IT guy can go now & everyone goes back on their merry way.

Months go by. You're still super busy trying to keep up with all the work you have going on. But everything has been totally fine with the computers. You haven't called your IT guy in a while because you haven't had any issues. Everything has been just fine.

Until the day your IT guy leaves the country for a vacation with his family.

"It's back," you exclaim on a phone call, "That red window from a few months back saying all my stuff is gone – it's back! What do I do now?"

I walk you through shutting down the ransomware (this particular strain allowed it) and letting me access your computer remotely. I start poking around to see how this happened again. This time you assured me you didn't click on anything.

Upon investigation (4000 miles away!), I'm able to find a few things that were left behind by your old IT guy. I won't bore you with the details but think: Remote Desktop to your server was open.

But wait – didn't this start with an email that you clicked, Johnny? How did they find open ports and attack your office?

The answer is simple and all too common nowadays. The hacking group that was able to trick you into opening their email and installing their malicious software came back. They were able to obtain your IP address from the first time they encrypted all your data. You never paid them, and they are angry about it. So, they came after you again!

And, this time, they did way more damage. Backups are deleted. Gone. Every computer on your network is infected with ransomware and all your files are encrypted. Again.

How do we even deal with this now? Do we pay the ransom? No, we never pay the ransom. In some cases, it is actually illegal now (at least in the US) to pay the ransom.

We do the only thing we can do: reinstall everything.

Everything gets a fresh installation of Windows, including the server. We found a backup on an external hard drive from 4-5 months ago, so we use that. We close all the ports your previous IT guy left open for his own access. This is really bad, Johnny.

After a few days of downtime, your company is back up and running. Woohoo! But – not so fast. You're missing 4-5 months-worth of data. That means your staff now has to rebuild your accounting data for the past 4-5 months. Do you have all the invoices you've sent to customers printed out and saved, Johnny? Do you have every bill you paid filed away somewhere so you can re-enter them? This sounds like a lot of work, and believe me, it is.

Are you freaked out yet? Imagine this happened to you. How much money would you lose? How do you rebuild 4-5 months-worth of accounting data which you have no other records of? Most companies that experience a hack (or reoccurring hack, like this one) go out of business very quickly.

The story I just told you is based upon a true story that I experienced with one of my customers a number of years ago. A tired, busy business owner clicked something he shouldn't have. One-click cost them a week of downtime and about 6 months of extra work to re-do what was lost. Luckily, they did not close-up shop and did have some paper records which they were able to duplicate in their computer systems. Both the customer and I learned a lot from this situation.

In an age where computers and the internet are vital to almost every business' daily functions, companies cannot be allowed to skimp on IT and security due to lack of knowledge and understanding or because the owner is cheap. This is something that my company takes seriously, and we now make a seemingly over asserted effort to educate our customers and potential customers in cybersecurity best practices. A few simple things can prevent large attacks like this from gaining any ground at all.

One-off IT guys are a thing of the past. At my company, we actually refuse to operate this way now. A small business that has no IT staff can no longer skate by managing their own IT and calling in the pros only when they think they need to. A business owner generally does not have the necessary technical knowledge to handle this well, if at all. At my company, we offer all-inclusive flat-rate solutions to help small businesses manage their cyber risk and help them to grow and manage their business using technology efficiently. That also means that we have some skin in the game, and we care about protecting our customers. We don't just pick up the phone when they call but we have the flexibility to proactively do things without worrying about charging the customer for the work. It's simply included. This allows us to provide certain protections that would most likely have protected Johnny from the Ransomware attack – twice.

There is a bare minimum of security tools necessary to be used in a business, which is today a considerably higher standard than maybe 2-3 years ago. Anti-Virus alone does not cut it anymore.

In summary, the cyber threat landscape today is vastly different and much more vicious than it has ever been. Computers are still 'new' as compared to the history of the world and there is much to do to ensure we are using them in a secure fashion and to keep up with the ever-evolving threat landscape. Businesses small and large must take great care and make it a priority to secure their technology equipment.

Security alone, however, is not the answer. You must train your staff! Just as we take the time for mandated state sexual harassment training, cybersecurity training is equally important. Employees (and owners!) need to have the skillset to recognize what is real and what is fake in their inbox.

Imagine that your IT service provider is just part of the fabric of your business, rather than a vendor that "helps you out sometimes."

Imagine that you avoid the entire situation described in Johnny's story because you care about your cybersecurity risk and invest to protect yourself from it, and you have an IT service provider who really cares about this stuff. Your IT service provider is doing all they can to prevent any real threats from actually getting to you. Inevitably, something always comes through. But there they are, stepping in and training you and your employees regularly about the evolving threats and how to spot them and stop them.

Imagine that instead of your accounting department rebuilding data from the past 5 months, your company is operating 'business as usual' and you didn't even get hacked.

Imagine that evening at 10 pm when you were checking your email trying to open a bank statement that your IT company received some notifications about the file you were trying to run. The next morning, they call to inform you of what happened and that their security tools were able to stop it from causing any damage to your network. Imagine that.

Imagine this actually to be possible. Because it is! As threats are evolving rapidly so is IT Security and the tools that are used to do it. All you need to do is a few basic things: Protect, Train, Adapt. With the help of a trusted provider, all of this is possible and easier, and more cost-effective than you think. Don't be a 'Johnny one-click' who destroys your entire company with a click of a button. Be Cyber Smart!

About the Author

Joseph A. Vitti is the founder & CEO of Impetra Technology Solutions LLC in Stamford, Connecticut. He began his career at a young age as a Linux systems administrator and later moved into a DevOps role. In 2015, he began Impetra Technology Solutions LLC, a Managed Services Provider, driven to bring business owners handcrafted cybersecurity solutions with unmatched quality and technical excellence. We help our customers stay safe on the computer, offline, and in the cloud, and teach them how to use technology to grow and scale their business.

Check out our FREE Guide - 5 ways to be Cyber Smart at Work. https://5ways.impetra.com.

How to Protect
Your Data

By Tim Smoot

Many things in life are simple but not easy. Take losing weight. The concept is quite simple, just eat less and exercise more, right? Implementing that and having success can be another story altogether. Sometimes we have the best intentions but simply don't do what is required and therefore have little success. You are probably asking yourself by now, "Tim this is supposed to be a Cyber Security book, where are we going with this?" While this scenario does apply to dieting, it also applies to Cyber Security.

Most clients and future clients I speak to have one major thing in common. They believe securing their data is an easy process. Many think it is some fancy new piece of hardware that just magically does everything, like a big shiny new lock to put on the door. Unfortunately, that could not be further from the truth. Like the great philosopher Shrek once said, "Ogres are like onions" and explained that they have many layers. Much like ogres, securing your data also needs to have layers to be effective. No one piece of equipment or software will magically do it for you. It is hard work and must be done with great care.

There are many different angles to take on this topic but for this chapter, we will look at it through the eyes of an

131

organization's CEO. We will take 30,000-foot view and apply it to an entire organization. In reality, the whole book could be dedicated to this topic and could contain thousands of pages. That much detail would be overwhelming and very hard to digest. To communicate as much information as clearly as possible, we will break it all into seven layers.

1. Have a Plan

To be truly prepared you must look at the situation from all angles. Writing out a plan will help provide clarity on what data you have and where it is stored, and therefore what must be done to secure it. This plan should provide a holistic view of your organization's data and the protections being put into place. This plan should also encompass the "what if's" and how you would respond to any number of situations. In addition to having the plan, you must have your team practice the plan. While having a theory on how to get your business back up and running is a good start it should also be tested. If your internal team or external support company is not doing this, make them or start looking for their replacements.

2. Protect Against Malware

Viruses and other malicious software are a huge threat and much more common than you think. They can do a massive amount of damage including everything from data loss or compromise, to severe financial consequences and in some industries, it can even cost you licensure. Within this area, several things come together for this protection. First, an enterprise-grade firewall with a current security subscription must be in place. Regardless of what they advertise, there is not a sufficient firewall in your cable modem.

Second, deploy a next generation antivirus. We like the offering from Sentinel One. The difference between this and a conventional antivirus is that it does not depend on the list of known viruses that conventional options use. This makes Sentinel One much better at catching new or evolving threats.

Finally, deploy email protection. Many of the threats to your organization arrive via email. Keeping this secured is one of the keys to any malware control strategy.

3. Secure Your Wireless

Your wireless can be an easy way in for hackers if you allow it to be. People often forget about wireless security or they don't give it the attention they should. With a couple of simple steps, you can minimize the risk. Set the encryption on your network to the highest standard that your hardware supports. While any level of encryption can be broken, the harder you make it the better. Turn off the broadcasting of your wireless network name. This keeps it from being an obvious target as you can't hack what you don't know is there. We also suggest that you keep your guest network physically segregated from your company network. Allow guests internet access through the guest network but keep them off of your main network.

4. Secure Your Passwords

Even something so simple can make a huge security difference. I'm sure you have heard the importance of passwords many times. That is for good reason because they are that important. Having weak passwords can put your data and organization at risk. Make your passwords at least 10-12 characters and include capital and small letters, numbers, and special characters. The more random the characters seem, the more secure it is. Don't share your passwords with anyone, not even your IT department. If they are asking you for them, they do not know how to do their job properly. Don't save all of your passwords to your computer. While this can make life easy it also is a huge risk. Finally, don't reuse passwords for multiple things and be sure to change them often. To help with this we suggest the use of a password manager app. This type of app stores all your passwords and keeps them accessible yet safe.

5. Keep Thing Up to Date

Running updates, especially those long ones for Microsoft Windows, can be a pain. This is a pain that must be accepted to keep your organization safe. Your IT provider should be able to do this after hours to keep it from affecting productivity during the workday. The same care should be taken on all software and devices used to make sure all apps and operating systems are kept up to date. These updates are often mostly comprised of fixes to security holes. If the holes are not fixed, they can be exploited by hackers.

6. Backup Everything

Backups are arguably the most important item on this list. In today's world, it's not a matter of if something will happen to you but more a matter of when. Having every possible protection in place can certainly minimize risk but nothing is 100% effective. Backups help ensure that your organization is ready for anything and will survive an attack. When it comes to backups, not all are created equal. Many people think backing up to a thumb drive is all they need. That could not be further from the truth. Here at We Secure Inc., we believe that the more points of failure that can be removed in any process the better off we are. Backing up your data must be automated, often, and not just a single copy. We use a product from Intronis that backs you up 3 times over. There is a local appliance located on your site that copies your files and stores them locally. This device then pushes the data securely over the Internet to multiple cloud locations providing redundancy in your backups. This device can also backup things you may store on another provider such as Office 365 for your email. This makes sure you have a copy of your data that cannot be deleted regardless of what happens in Microsoft's cloud.

7. Educate Everyone

Everything that we have covered so far is very important but without adding this it would be difficult to remain secure. Most hacks and breaches have an element of human error in them. Whether it's acting on a fraudulent email or clicking a link to a dangerous website, human error accounts for the initiation of most hacks, breaches, and other issues. Having a formal education program is the key to getting and keeping your employees up to speed on the threats to your organization's data. Without knowing what the threats are it is difficult to avoid them. Having a solid system in place provides certainty in knowing that all employees have been trained in the same manner with the same information.

This likely seems overwhelming. You are correct, it is. The information provided in this chapter is only the tip of the iceberg in what is needed to keep your organization's data safe. This was only a 30,000-foot view and not all the data you need. It is intended to get you thinking about what your company is doing, and what they are not doing. Hopefully, you recognized many of these items because you already do them.

If you need help, starting that process is just a click away. Go to wesecureinc.com and make an appointment for a complimentary 30-minute consultation with me or one of my team. We would be happy to help in any way we can.

I'm often asked why I am so passionate about helping small businesses protect themselves. The answer is simple: I don't want to see another small business go through what so many have. will leave you with one simple request: talk to someone and find out exactly what position your business is in. By someone, I don't mean your copier company that also does IT support. Find a cybersecurity expert who can give you an expert opinion on the current security of your data. Let's talk soon.

About the Author

Tim Smoot is Executive Vice President of We Secure Cyber Security, a Cyber Security and IT Support provider. Tim brings to the table 32 years of experience in the IT industry holding many different positions over the years in various organizations. His diversified experience allows him a unique perspective and the ability view problems in a holistic manner.

Tim's team at We Secure take great pride in helping businesses stay safe and secure while supporting all of their IT needs.

You can connect with Tim online at:
https://www.linkedin.com/in/timsmoot

and connect with We Secure Inc. at:
https://www.facebook.com/wesecureinc